YOU'LL BE OLD SOMEDAY, TOO

RICHARD WORTH

YOU'LL
BE
OLD
SOMEDAY,
TOO

A GROLIER COMPANY

Franklin Watts 1986
New York London Toronto Sydney

Photographs courtesy of: UPI/Bettmann Newsphotos:
pp. 4, 26, 34, 36, 41, 42, 51, 67, 84, 96, 108; H.U.D.:
pp. 18, 21, 32, 71, 75, 78, 101; Charles Harbutt/
Archive Pictures Inc.: p. 27; The Bettmann Archive:
p. 45; Florida Division of Tourism: p. 93.

Library of Congress Cataloging in Publication Data
Worth, Richard.
You'll be old someday, too.
Bibliography: p.
Includes index.
Summary: Explores current attitudes toward aging
and the elderly in the United States. Also includes
interviews with retirees from various parts of the
country discussing how they are managing their lives.
1. Aged—United States—Social conditions—Juvenile
literature.   2. Aged—United States—Economic conditions
—Juvenile literature.   3. Retirement—United States—
Juvenile literature.   [1. Aged]   I. Title.
HQ1064.U5W68   1986   305.2′6   85-29419
ISBN 0-531-10158-4

CONTENTS

YOU'LL BE OLD SOMEDAY, TOO

INTRODUCTION

Old age concerns everyone. Most of us who are young today will be old someday ourselves; our parents will grow old even sooner; and our grandparents or great-grandparents have probably reached old age already. So it's important that we know something about the experience of old age not only for ourselves and our relatives but for the millions of elderly who live in America today.

Thus, *You'll Be Old Someday, Too* has a two-fold purpose. First, it tries to present a realistic picture of the condition of old people in our society. To do this, the book begins with a historical perspective that provides some explanation of our current attitudes toward old age. It also examines the general circumstances in which old people find themselves—their income, housing, health, and family life—as well as their view of themselves and the world around them.

The second purpose of the book is to start each of us thinking seriously about the question: What kind of old age will I have? To provide a few answers, I interviewed a variety of old people. Some were tired and depressed. But many others led active and interesting lives. I met an older woman in Florida who hosts her own radio and TV programs; a man in Connecticut who began a second career after his retirement; and a woman from Maryland who discovered that she possessed quite a flair for writing. Each of their stories is here, and there are thousands more in America just like them.

What I've learned has helped me form a positive image of what my old age can be. I hope it will do the same for you.

CHAPTER ONE

OLD AGE:
A PERSPECTIVE

In an interview given just before his death, the great photographer Ansel Adams looked back over his long and brilliant career. Adams readily described himself as a "workaholic," for even at the age of eighty-two he was still putting in a full day either in the field or in the darkroom. He reminisced freely about his friends, among them the celebrated artist Georgia O'Keefe, whom he had once photographed; as well as the people who had influenced his development as a photographer. One of the most important of these influences, Adams admitted, came when he traveled with his family to Yosemite National Park as a youth in 1916. This was really the start of his career, for Yosemite became the inspiration for so many of his timeless photographs. During the course of the interview, Adams characterized his entire life as a "constant state of searching awareness." Through this awareness, he preserved for all time the vistas of the American West and transformed photography into the art that it is today.

Even for a man as active as Ansel Adams, old age was still an occasion to pause and look back—to sum up and gain perspective on life. It is the same for many people as they reach old age, whether their lives have been marked by uncommon achievements or simply those common events that will fill most of our lives.

Perhaps it is appropriate, then, to begin this discussion of old age by trying to gain some perspective on aging. By looking at old people in past societies, we can understand more clearly our present attitudes toward aging and realize why we regard old people the way we do. Looking backward at the life of an individual or an entire society can tell us where we are and how we got here.

LOOKING BACKWARD

From culture to culture, attitudes toward old age have differed. There is not too much information regarding these attitudes in the ancient world. One reason is that few people ever reached old age. Fatal diseases, unhealthy diet, poor sanitation, as well as constant warfare, were causes of early death. In the ancient world, reaching old age meant celebrating your sixtieth birthday, but less than 20 percent of the population was ever lucky enough to do so.

Among the ancient Maya Indians, whose civilization arose in Central America about 1500 B.C., the aged were held in great esteem because of their wisdom and experience. In this culture, old people continued to hunt or till the fields to teach the young how these things were done. They also passed down traditional songs and tribal myths,

Photographer Ansel Adams
when he was 80 years old.
Adams believed in hard work
and planned never to retire.

and conducted adolescents through the ceremonial rites-of-passage into adulthood. The aged would continue to hold their important places in this society as long as they were competent to do so. But once they lost their wits and were no longer useful, they were cast out and left to die.

Among the ancient Greeks, old people were highly respected and held positions of great authority. As an example, many of the ancient Greek city-states had a *gerusia*, or council of elders, which helped run the government. But while old people were held in high regard, old age itself was often seen as a great burden because of its effects on the body. As the Greek poet Menander (c. 342–291 B.C.) wrote:

> *O burdensome old age! You have nothing good to offer mortals, but you are lavish with pain and disease. And yet we all hope to reach you, and we do our very best to succeed.*

About three centuries later, the ancient Roman poet Ovid wrote this unfavorable description of an old woman:

> *. . . this beauty will become the prey of pitiless old age which is creeping up silently, step by step. They will say she was beautiful.*

A far more positive view of old age was written by another Roman—the senator and orator, Marcus Tullius Cicero. In *De Senectute (On Old Age)*, which was written when he was sixty-three, Cicero sets down some of the reasons why people think old age is a burden and then he rebuts them. While admitting that old age weakens the body, Cicero points out that active exercise and temperance can help it retain some of its strengths. Old age does deprive us of much physical pleasure, Cicero says, but this only allows us to concentrate more of our energies on intellectual pursuits. Finally, Cicero points out that old age does not have to remove us from active involvement in life.

The great affairs of life are not performed by physical strength, or activity . . . but by deliberation, character, expression of opinion. Of these old age is not only not deprived, but as a rule, has them in greater degree. . . . The mightiest states have been brought into peril by young men [and] have been supported and restored by old.

In the ancient world, most people seemed to hold two views of growing old that appear to be in conflict with each other. The elderly were held in high regard for their wisdom and experience; at the same time, people felt that aging was still a difficult ordeal because of the pain and disease that came with it. These conflicting views continued to be held from ancient times until the modern era.

OLD AGE IN AMERICA

We know from their writings that the Puritan colonists held old people in great esteem just as the ancients did. To the Puritans, old people were among the elect, those especially chosen by God for an honored place in Heaven. As the Puritan preacher Increase Mather wrote, "If any man is favored with long life, it is God that has lengthened his days." One reason old people may have seemed so singly favored was that there were so few of them. During the colonial period, the average life expectancy was about thirty, and less than 2 percent of the population lived to be elderly, that is sixty or over.

Those fortunate enough to reach old age were treated by the Puritans with great respect. Old people were accorded the best seats in church. The churches, themselves, were actually run by groups of elders who served for life. And elderly leaders routinely filled the most important positions of government. For as Increase Mather put it:

It is presumed that old men know more than younger ones. Aged persons are fittest to give

counsel . . . fittest to be trusted with the greatest
and most honorable offices.

Retirement in the colonies was almost unknown, and
leaders routinely served until death. Roger Williams, for
example, remained a powerful force in the affairs of Rhode
Island until he died at almost eighty. William Byrd of
Westover battled a host of infirmities that beset him in
old age but still continued active in the political events of
his native Virginia. At the age of eighty, Deacon Josiah
Haynes participated in the fighting at Concord on April 19,
1775. Haynes then joined in pursuing the British redcoats
back to Boston, where he was cut down by a bullet along
the way. But perhaps the best known example of a man
remaining active into old age was Benjamin Franklin, who
helped write the Declaration of Independence, served as
American ambassador to France, and participated in the
Constitutional Convention, all after he had passed the age
of sixty-five. For many Americans, Franklin seemed to con-
firm the cherished belief that old age and worldly wisdom
went hand in hand.

In addition to their power in church and state, old
people were a significant force in the economic life of the
colonies. They ran family businesses in towns and villages,
and participated in trading ventures. Aged patriarchs were
also known to hold onto their land until they were near
death, refusing to divide it up among their sons. This
undoubtedly led to hostility between the generations, although there is little evidence that it was ever expressed
openly.

Nevertheless, old people did come in for at least some
public criticism. Even as conservative a leader as Cotton
Mather said:

Old age is often too covetous, too sparing, too
hoarding and ready to lay up . . . old folks often
seem to grasp the hardest for the world, when they
are just going out of it: an evil release.

And William Bridge, in his *Word to the Aged,* wrote that old people were "apt to be too touchy, peevish, angry and forward . . . hard to please . . . full of complaints . . . uncharitable to the sins of youth." Clearly the Puritans were not blind to the fact that old people had their faults just like everybody else.

Toward the end of the eighteenth century a marked change seems to have begun in the position occupied by old people in society. Some historians believe this was due to the combined effects of the American and French Revolutions, which spread the ideas of liberty and equality. People challenged the establishment and those who ruled it—whether they were aristocrats, a colonial power, or the aged.

No longer did the elderly so routinely receive preferred treatment. (Of course, such treatment had never been given to the aged poor. They were generally regarded as outcasts.) Between 1750 and 1830, for example, New England churches gradually stopped giving the best seats to their eldest members; these were now reserved for the wealthiest. American state legislatures, between 1790 and 1820, decreed a mandatory retirement age for judges and other officeholders. A change in fashion also symbolized a greater emphasis on youth. In the past men had worn white wigs, which made them look older. But these fell out of favor, and men began using hair dyes to give themselves a younger appearance. Clothes also came into fashion which favored the slim, shapelier bodies of younger men. Finally, historians have pointed out that the number of negative terms used to describe old people increased— words such as "codger," "fuddy-duddy," "geezer," and "old timer."

Some leaders, such as John Adams, deplored the changes that were occurring in America. But his longtime political rival Thomas Jefferson disagreed. He was firmly convinced that the young should not be controlled by the old. These sentiments were later echoed by Henry David Thoreau in *Walden.*

Age is no better, hardly so well, qualified for an instructor as youth, for it has not profitted so much as it has lost. Practically, the old have no very important advice to give. . . .

Although the poet Henry Wadsworth Longfellow regarded old age as a period of decline, he offers a more balanced view of it.

Whatever poet, orator, or sage may say of it, old age is still old age.
It is the waning, not the crescent moon;
The dusk of evening, not the blaze of noon
For age is opportunity no less
Than youth itself, though in another dress
And as the evening twilight fades away
The sky is filled with stars,
invisible by day.

As Longfellow's words were written, America was undergoing an Industrial Revolution. This would bring great changes to society, affecting the lives of almost everyone, including the elderly. Industrialization required new knowledge and new skills. The wisdom of old people, based on years of past experience, was therefore not as important as it once had been. Among middle-class families, the elderly still held a valued place. But their advice may have seemed less and less relevant to young people who were trying to make their way in a world that was changing rapidly and becoming far different from anything their elders had known.

During the course of the Industrial Revolution some of these young people would become successful entrepreneurs, like John D. Rockefeller and J.P. Morgan. As old men, they would be greatly admired and respected. However, this was not because of their age but because they were rich and powerful.

For the millions who worked for Rockefeller or Morgan, old age would be something quite different. Industrialization had a way of grinding people down and making them old long before their time. Twelve hours a day, six days a week, in a woolen mill or a meat-packing plant was enough to break any man or woman. By the turn of the century, mandatory retirement had become the standard practice in many industries. But when older people retired, they were condemned to poverty because they had no other source of income except their wages. It was estimated that around 1910, 30 to 40 percent of the elderly were dependent on charity from their communities, families, or friends. Interviews conducted during the period indicated that many old people were afraid of being a burden on their children or, worse, dying in the poor-house. At these dreary places, they were given enough food to survive and a hard bed on which to sleep. Before long, however, they were dead, and their bodies were buried in potter's field—the final resting place of the poor and anonymous.

By the beginning of the twentieth century some companies, such as U.S. Steel and Standard Oil, had instituted pension programs. But these covered only a small number of workers, and they could be revoked without notice whenever the company might decide to do so. Americans were reluctant to take a much larger step and follow the example of many European governments that had already installed a system of compulsory old-age insurance. To many, this idea represented socialism and government interference, and went against the true spirit of American individualism. As far as American public opinion was concerned, people who wanted government handouts were lazy, shiftless souls who deserved nothing.

As the century wore on, however, these attitudes gradually changed. One reason was the increasing number of old people, probably due to such things as improved diet and advances in medicine. Where only about one-third of all

Americans had reached their sixtieth birthday in 1830, that number had grown to one-half in 1900, and would reach two-thirds by 1940. However, large numbers of these old people were living in poverty, too many for America to keep ignoring much longer.

By 1930, some states had already passed old-age pension laws, while others provided assistance for the aged poor. Various schemes had also been proposed to provide old-age pensions for everyone over the age of sixty. But more than any other single factor, it was the Great Depression that made the concept of old-age insurance acceptable to large numbers of the American population. It now became clear that poverty was not simply the result of laziness; it could happen to anyone, even hardworking citizens.

Finally, in 1935 the Social Security Act was passed by Congress. It was a conservative measure, designed to provide only some income for retired workers and their families; the rest would have to come from other sources. But, at least, millions of aged Americans would no longer be forgotten. Upon the passage of the Social Security Act, President Franklin Roosevelt stated:

If the Senate and the House of Representatives in this long and arduous session had done nothing more than pass this Bill, the session would be regarded as historic for all time.

The establishment of social security marked the beginning of a new era for the elderly—one which has continued to the present day. How does this era compare to those that came before?

Today, people are no longer held in high regard simply because of their old age as they were in the ancient world or in Colonial America. While many old people still hold positions of authority in politics and cultural affairs as they did in the past, the majority have retired from an active involvement in the workplace. Nevertheless, America no longer abandons its retired people as it did in so many cases less than a century ago. Today, there is not only social security, but various pension programs as well.

Yet, while we certainly care about the elderly, we no longer look to them for their experience and advice as much as people did in the past. Younger men and women now run things pretty much on their own. Frequently, the elderly act only as observers.

CHAPTER TWO

THE AGED
IN AMERICA

In America today, we idolize youth; in this respect, our society is no different from some earlier cultures. What does seem different, however, is the degree to which we are obsessed with being young. Perhaps it is partly the fault of the media, for no other culture has ever before been inundated by so many messages in the form of advertisements and entertainment. The media has contributed mightily to the creation of the youth cult.

Sexy young men and women are spread across the covers of magazines and the front pages of the tabloids. Inside are more young people selling us every type of product imaginable—from underarm deodorant to exotic Caribbean vacations. Television also features young people in commercials, daytime soap operas, and nighttime serials. All ages seem to worship at the fountain of youth, and the desire to stay eternally young has become an obsession. Americans purchase hair dyes to wash the gray away; apply vast quantities of makeup to hide the wrinkles; even submit to facelifts and tummy tucks, just to keep old age from snaring us. In contrast to this infatuation with youth, we often view old age and old people with despair. Sadly, all the old people who have subscribed to the youth cult during most of their lives finally become the victims of it. And those who are young today will eventually become its victims, too.

Why have we done this to ourselves? In part, we have come to believe a lot of things about old age that are simply untrue. In this chapter and those that follow, we will examine the realities of old age and try to separate them from the myths.

THE ELDERLY POPULATION

At present, 27 million people in America are sixty-five or older; and their numbers are confidently predicted to climb to 35 million by the year 2000. This compares to only about 3 million elderly in 1900, and a little over 12 million in 1950. So you can see that the elderly population has mushroomed in recent years, at the very time when the birth rate has been declining. As a result, the elderly now comprise almost 12 percent of the American people, and that could increase to 22 percent by the year 2030. This has led to the so-called "graying of America," a phenomenon which is occurring in other highly industrialized Western nations as well.

There are several reasons why more people are now living into an old age than ever before. Diet and sanitation conditions have improved, and medical science has conquered many diseases—diphtheria and measles, for example —that once kept life expectancy low. More recently, medicine has also achieved significant advances against three modern killers: heart disease, stroke, and cancer.

A sample of the population reveals that women generally outlive men. At present, a white female baby born in 1980 is expected to live to age seventy-eight; a white male baby to age seventy. And the gap continues to widen.

Why do women live longer? Genetics probably plays a role. Women have also been far less prone to develop certain cancers or heart disease. But doctors hasten to point out that as more and more women have joined the ranks of cigarette smokers, the incidence of cancer among them has risen. With an increasing number of women entering the work force, they may also succumb to the pressures that contribute to heart disease. Nevertheless, sociologists have found that women are far more adept than men at forming meaningful relationships among their co-workers, which can help them deal with pressures on the job.

A further sampling of the population shows that whites in our society generally outlive blacks and other minorities. One reason is that many people in minority groups live in poverty, which is a more stressful condition. Blacks, for example, have more strokes than whites. In addition, poor people often cannot afford nutritious diets. Nevertheless, the difference in life expectancy between whites and minorities is narrowing, a trend expected to continue over the next fifty years.

Finally, a larger number of people are not only living into their sixties or early seventies, but a decade or so beyond. Today, men who celebrate their sixty-fifth birthday can expect to live until eighty; and women will reach eighty-four. In fact this increased longevity has led sociologists to separate the elderly into two distinct groups: the "young old," aged sixty-five to seventy-four; and the "old old," aged seventy-four and over.

ECONOMIC CONDITIONS

While the popular belief is that most old people are poor, in actuality many live in adequate or comfortable financial circumstances. Income, however, declines sharply in old age. A man, for example, frequently reaches the top of his career and enjoys peak earnings during his fifties and early

*An elderly woman receiving
information on proper nutrition*

sixties, only to have retirement bring a significant drop in his income. Because a married woman is often younger than her husband, she may continue working after he retires. But this income may not substantially improve a couple's financial situation because women often earn much less than men.

For most elderly couples, the primary source of income is social security, financed through payroll taxes paid by employees and employers. When social security became law in 1935, individuals could not begin receiving benefits until they reached sixty-five, the age of retirement. Today many people choose to retire early, at age sixty-two when, under subsequent amendments to the law, they can receive 80 percent of their benefits. Additionally, the law entitles a married woman who never worked to 50 percent of her husband's benefits. This usually comes to more money than the woman would have received if she had worked and received her own social security benefits, leading many working women to complain bitterly that they pay a lot in social security taxes and get very little in return. Since 1977, retirees have also been granted cost-of-living adjustments to their benefits—increases determined by the rate of inflation.

Aside from social security, about half of America's retired workers enjoy pension benefits. Some derive additional income from savings and investments. From all of these sources, the majority of elderly people can effectively maintain an adequate standard of living.

While income in old age remains adequate, if significantly reduced, some expenses undergo a significant reduction too. For example, 70 percent of the elderly own their own homes and most have entirely paid off their mortgages. Nevertheless, they must still bear the burden of real estate taxes and fuel bills. Additionally, there are the costs of running an automobile as well as expenditures for food and clothing. Ordinarily, clothing expenses have declined since the elderly are usually retired and no longer need to purchase clothes for work. The elderly are also generally spared the enormous costs of child-rearing, which ended for most of them years earlier.

One expense that increases is medical care, for as people age, they fall victim to longer and more serious illness. In 1965, Congress passed Medicare, a measure designed to provide medical benefits for those sixty-five and over. Part A of Medicare—paid for out of social security taxes—covers hospital costs as well as some types of care given to the elderly at home. But Medicare does not cover all the costs for an extended hospital visit and these can wipe out an individual's entire savings.

If the elderly want to be covered by Part B of Medicare, they must make monthly payments. Part B pays the bills for doctors as well as various out-patient services; but only up to 80 percent, the patient must pick up the rest. In addition, Medicare pays little or nothing for such essentials as prescriptions, regular dental care, eye exams and eyeglasses, routine foot care, private duty nurses in the hospital, or meals delivered to an old person's home if he or she is unable to prepare them.

Thus, while Medicare may offer extensive benefits, its coverage falls far short of total care. Elderly people must buy additional medical insurance, or cover the remaining costs out of their own pockets, which can prove financially devastating.

THE POOR

While the majority of the elderly receive adequate incomes, the story of old age in America is really a tale of two populations. Approximately 15 percent of the aged live below the poverty line, and at least as many more hover precariously just above it. A large number of the impoverished elderly are women, in part because they simply live longer than men. When her husband dies, a woman may not be entitled to continue receiving his pension bene-

The urban elderly poor often live in run-down cramped quarters because they cannot afford to live elsewhere.

fits, which pushes her beneath the poverty line. (Many women do not work long enough to qualify for pensions themselves.) Some women, who were divorced or deserted by their husbands and left to raise families on their own, may have spent most of their lives barely scraping by. Old age and poor health only worsen their circumstances. A high proportion of these women are blacks and other minorities.

In 1972, Congress authorized that the elderly poor should be granted additional financial support under the Supplemental Security Income program (SSI). Seven years later another, more widely known measure—Medicaid—was passed. This joint federal and state program pays for medical expenses such as hospital care, treatment by a physician, nursing homes, and other types of assistance that the elderly poor cannot afford.

But Medicaid or SSI do not provide an answer for all these poor. Some are much too proud to accept assistance, while for others assistance simply arrives too late. Many of these people have languished in poverty for an entire lifetime. Years may have passed since they last consulted a doctor; and their health has steadily deteriorated until little can be done to restore it. What's more, the poor often lack the telephones to even call a doctor, to say nothing of money for the transportation to get there, or for the special diet that the doctor may prescribe.

While most of the elderly poor live in cities, a large number can also be found in rural areas. Approximately 11 million aged live in rural America; an estimated 20 percent of them below the poverty line. For these aged, all the problems of being old and poor are simply magnified. The sense of isolation often increases, since much greater distances separate them from their nearest neighbors. Usually there is no public transportation, and they are too poor to afford a car. When they need medical care they must travel much farther to get it. At the same time, the elderly often tend to be fiercely independent and extremely suspicious of the government which seems far away in Washington or the state capital. And they are reluctant to look in that direction for any type of assistance. In addition, government programs often seem very confusing. Even when aid exists, it is often difficult to figure out what is available, or how it can be obtained. As a result, old people turn to friends or family, who can sometimes provide enough support. But, in other cases, friends have died off and families have moved away to the cities leaving the aged alone to fend for themselves.

HOUSING AMONG THE ELDERLY

Among the surprising statistics regarding the elderly is that the vast majority own the homes in which they live. This provides old people with a large measure of independence, something which they seem to value quite highly. Repeated surveys have shown that the major reason why many of the elderly live on their own, and not with their adult children, is simply that they prefer to. Of course, family members often live farther apart than they once did, making house-sharing between adult children and their elderly parents more difficult. In 1950, for example, 30 percent of the aged lived with their children; by 1980, this figure had dropped to 15 percent. Increased social security and pension benefits have made it easier than ever before for the elderly to retain their homes and their independence.

Nevertheless, as time goes on, an elderly person's home can become more and more expensive to maintain. Most elderly people own older homes which often need many repairs, and the cost of making them is usually quite high. In addition, they must deal with costly fuel bills and rising taxes. The price of independence can easily grow into a costly burden—too costly for the elderly to bear. In response to this situation, programs have been developed at the local, state, and federal levels that offer the elderly various forms of relief.

In Buffalo, New York, for instance, a program called HELP (Home Equity Living Plans) was started by the city with funds from the U.S. Department of Housing and Urban Development. Under this program, elderly residents are guaranteed lifetime use of their homes, but when they die, their homes become the property of HELP. In return HELP pays the property taxes, house insurance, and performs any necessary repairs while the elderly homeowners are still alive.

Communities such as Babylon, New York, and Portland, Oregon, permit elderly homeowners to convert 25 percent of their homes to create "accessory apartments." (In most residential areas such apartments are prohibited by zoning regulations.) By renting out an apartment, an elderly person can not only gain additional income but also obtain companionship, which may be just as important. In the early 1980s, an estimated 2.5 million of these "accessory apartments" existed coast to coast.

Another program, called Project Match, was started in San Jose, California during 1977. The project brings together elderly people who, for various reasons, are unable to maintain a home on their own. At first the program matched only the elderly in these house-sharing arrangements; but gradually, it expanded to include younger people, too. A young person who shares the house of an elderly resident often performs various household chores and provides extra security as well as needed companionship. Similar programs can be found in other communities throughout the country.

A different type of living arrangement available to some elderly people is government-subsidized congregate housing. In Hamden, Connecticut, for example, this type of housing is an option for residents whose income falls below a certain specified level. Apartment rents are kept low; an inexpensive meal is provided every day; and there is twenty-four-hour supervision, as well as various kinds of recreational activities. At present, the demand for this kind of housing among the elderly far exceeds the supply. In Great Britain, by contrast, more of it is currently available.

Instead of state-subsidized housing, many of the elderly poor find themselves living in cheap hotels located in the rundown sections of America's cities. Recent studies have shown that most of these hotel dwellers are men, who usually think of themselves as loners. They may have begun living on their own and traveling around the country from job to job as long ago as the Great Depression, when jobs were often difficult to find. Others who live in these hotels may be alcoholics or recent widowers. Since the hotels are located downtown, they are convenient to stores, restaurants, movie theaters, and public transportation. Old people seem able to survive in this type of environment, at least as long as their health holds out. When their health goes, they must be institutionalized.

By contrast, the more affluent elderly enjoy a far different life-style, many of them in retirement communities such as Sun City, Arizona. Sun City offers a variety of recreational activities, including golf, bowling, swimming and crafts. The homes are beautiful. The weather is warm and dry during much of the year, and none of the residents can be under fifty. As a result Sun City and other retirement communities have been accused of age segregation. But most of the people who live there seem to prefer the company of people their own age.

Another concept in elderly housing is the "life-care facility." This generally consists of an apartment complex, offering meals, recreational activities, and medical care. To move into these facilities, elderly people must be able to afford a large down payment which generally comes from the sale of their homes. In addition, there is a monthly charge, usually paid from social security benefits, pensions, or other sources of income. Life-care facilities will consider only those elderly people who enjoy relatively good health and can care for themselves, at least most of the time. Doctors are readily available, however, should residents

An aerial view of Sun City, Arizona

The dining room of a "life-care" facility

need them. Each apartment may also be equipped with a "panic button" that a resident can push in case of emergency. As residents' health declines to the point that they can no longer care for themselves, they automatically enter a convalescent home, which is part of the life-care facility. Patients pay for these services out of their remaining income; and, when this runs out, Medicaid takes over. The convalescent home will provide the patients with all necessary treatment until they die: thus, the term "life-care."

To learn more about life-care facilities, I traveled to a handsome high-rise complex in southern Connecticut to have lunch with two of the residents, Virginia and May (the mother of one of my close friends). May, who had been living in the facility for about six weeks, suffers from Parkinson's disease, a nerve disorder. The disease had already slowed May's step noticeably and made her look older and much frailer than her years. Virginia had moved into the complex about a year earlier, following the death of her husband. The couple had been married for forty years, and among their most prized possessions was the historic home which they had lovingly restored. After her husband's death, however, Virginia decided to sell it.

"Someone," she said, "asked me if I cried when I left the house. No, I told them, that part of my life is over. It was wonderful, but it's now over."

We ate lunch in a large, sunny dining room where the residents take all of their meals. Most of them are women alone like Virginia and May. The residents are required to eat together as a way of preventing them from remaining isolated in their apartments and to encourage the development of new friendships. The food was extremely well prepared and pleasantly served by an efficient group of waitresses who seemed genuinely interested in catering to the needs of the residents.

In addition to daily meals, the life-care facility provides a variety of recreational activities and other services. After lunch, May had an appointment to have her hair done; and Virginia was heading off for an afternoon game of bridge. Virginia also maintained her own car at the facility so she could leave to visit friends, run errands, or go shopping.

Before leaving for her hair appointment, May introduced me to another of her acquaintances, a plump, round-faced woman named Christina. She took me for a brief tour of the facility, pointing out where all the activities were held, including crafts, exercise classes, and feature-length movies. Christina also showed me the small garden plots which many of the residents, including herself, had planted. One woman we met had recently decided to give up her plot—apparently it had become too much for her to maintain—and she was still looking for someone to take over the care of her cherished rhubarb plants.

As we continued around the grounds, Christina explained why she had moved to the facility from her home in a condominium complex outside Detroit. "I thought I was doing quite well on my own," she said. "But my daughters live on the east coast and they worried about my being alone. The question was: What to do with mother?" Christina explained. And the decision was finally reached that Christina should come east to live where she could be closer to her daughters.

"I could understand that," Christina continued, "because I had faced the same thing with my mother."

Christina then commented on how amazed she was to see that so many of the residents of the life-care center lived to such advanced ages. She thought it must be because everything was provided for them there, and they were "protected from life's stresses."

As a final stop on our tour, Christina took me to the convalescent hospital, a clean modern facility where residents go when their health deteriorates. She said a variety of activities were provided for the patients. (At the time of our visit, however, none were in progress, and most of the patients remained in their rooms behind closed doors.)

At a life-care facility, the convalescent hospital offers the final reassurance that everything possible will be done to help you; and, as Christina said, you will be "protected from life's stresses." Yet it also seemed to be a sad reminder for all the more vigorous residents, like Christina herself, of the final outcome which awaited each of them.

NURSING HOMES

To most of us, nursing homes represent a fate that seems almost worse than death itself. Approximately 5 percent of the elderly reside in nursing homes; although a total of 20 percent will spend some time in these facilities before they die. Nursing homes conjure up images of abandonment, abuse, loss of respect and dignity. How real are these images?

In the 1970s, serious abuses were uncovered in the nursing home industry, and widespread reports circulated of patients being severely mistreated. Since that time, conditions have somewhat improved due to stricter government regulations and better training of nurses. But serious problems still remain. Nurses' aides, who are responsible for most of the routine care, are still undertrained and woefully underpaid. In many nursing homes, patients still have very little to occupy their time and spend most of the day stuck in their rooms staring at the television set. Nursing homes also represent institutional living, which means a loss of independence and privacy. Most of the residents, however, are probably too ill to continue living on their own.

While problems still exist, there are, nevertheless, many fine nursing homes throughout the country. At these facilities, the staffs are truly involved with their patients. They offer programs that provide the elderly with intellectual stimulation as well as physical exercise. And the elderly patients are not cut off from the rest of the community, but remain a part of it as much as possible.

A convalescent home in Gainesville, Florida, for example, participates in a nationwide program called RSVP (Retired Senior Volunteer Program). Residents in the home do mailings for community organizations and carry on voter registration drives among the other patients. They also serve as a welcoming committee for new residents and deliver mail throughout the facility. Such programs can be found in other nursing homes, too.

Over the past few years, the cost of nursing home care has skyrocketed. Generally, the elderly person who enters a nursing home will exhaust his or her savings in only a short time. When these are gone, Medicaid takes over. Since some of the elderly regard Medicaid as a form of welfare, it may be very difficult for them to accept this situation, especially if they have been self-supporting and independent all their lives. Critics also charge that because Medicaid pays nursing home charges but will not pay for many home health care services, a number of the elderly who could remain at home are forced to enter nursing facilities.

By contrast, Western European countries, such as Great Britain and Denmark, place a much greater emphasis on providing in-home care that will help elderly people remain within the community as long as possible. The British policy, for example, is that the "underlying principle of our services for the old should be this: that the best place for old people is their homes, with help from the home service if need be." We will look more closely at health care for the elderly in Chapter Six.

POLITICS

With their numbers growing rapidly, the elderly have become a potent force in American politics. A larger percentage of the aged votes than other age groups, and the aged write more letters to their elected representatives about the issues that concern them.

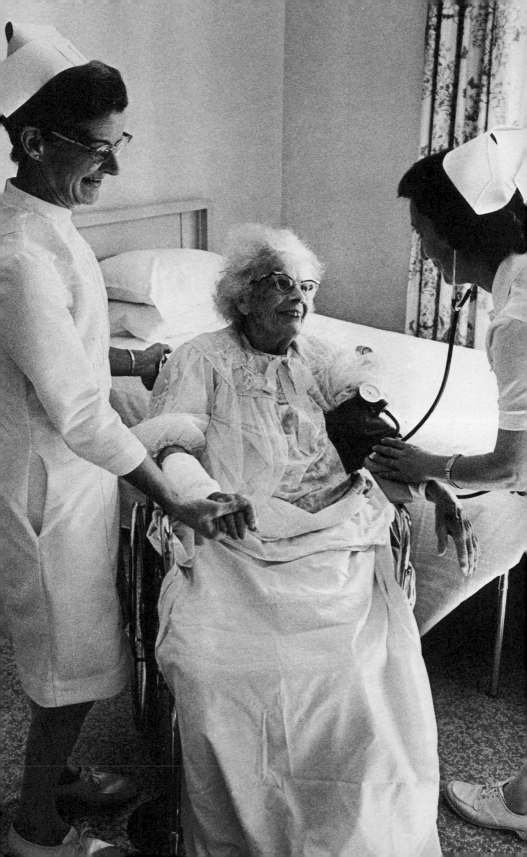

While it is not true that the elderly always vote as a bloc, they have been instrumental in achieving passage of important legislation at the local, state, and national level. This has included community programs to provide transportation for the elderly, and help them pay their utility bills. The aged also tend to vote against many local measures that might increase their property taxes.

In national politics the aged—through their lobbying efforts—have helped win congressional approval of Medicare and Medicaid, cost of living adjustments for social security, the SSI program, and a change in the mandatory retirement age from sixty-five to seventy. The increasing costs of these programs, however, have created mounting concern on Capitol Hill.

Social security is an example. Today, retired people are likely to receive far more in social security benefits than they paid into the program during their working years. The cost of these benefits is shouldered by younger workers who must pay higher and higher social security taxes. What's more, at the same time that the number of elderly retirees is growing, the number of younger workers in America is declining. This makes the burden even heavier. There is also a growing fear that the social security system may be unable to continue paying benefits at the present rate, thus jeopardizing the livelihoods of many younger workers when they reach retirement age.

There have been numerous calls to reform the system, but so far very little has been done because of the political issues involved. In 1983, Congress voted to tax the social security benefits of retired people whose total income exceeded a certain level. Social security taxes were also

A nursing home patient having her blood pressure taken

*Senior citizens demonstrating
against proposed government cuts
in social security benefits, 1982*

raised substantially for self-employed people. Meanwhile the Reagan administration tried to grapple with the exploding costs of health care. Medicare co-payments were increased. Hospitals were also required to charge a fixed fee set by the government for each of their medical procedures, rather than whatever seemed reasonable. Critics fear, however, that the fixed fee system may negatively affect many patients. Let's say a hospital charges more than the fixed fee for the costs of an operation, which includes the cost of keeping a patient in a room during the recovery period. The hospital might discharge a patient early, before he or she is really well enough to leave, so that all the costs for the operation will be covered by the fixed fee.

Over the years, threats to change the existing benefit system have met with vigorous opposition from the elderly through their organizations. The largest of these groups, the American Association of Retired Persons (AARP), has over 19 million members throughout the country. AARP conducts a potent lobbying effort in Washington, and it can mount a powerful letter-writing campaign among its members whenever an important issue arises. The elderly who belong to the association receive attractive group health insurance rates; discounts on medicines, hotels, and car rentals; as well as the AARP magazines. The association also carries on extensive research into the problems and concerns of the aged.

Another prominent organization is the Gray Panthers, founded in 1970 by Margaret Kuhn and some of her associates. Considered more outspoken than the AARP, the Panthers have resorted to picketing and demonstrations to express their views on issues ranging from the Vietnam War to nursing homes. The Gray Panthers see themselves as more than simply a group of old people exclusively supporting the interests of the aged. Their mission is to fight against ageism as it relates to young and old. As Margaret Kuhn explains:

We will not use our large numbers and our growing political awareness exclusively for our own self-interest or to build another self-serving group. Old people as elders of the tribe should be . . . safeguarding the survival of the tribe—the larger public interest.

This chapter has presented an overview of America's aged, focusing on aspects such as the enormous increase in this segment of the population as well as their extended longevity. Economic conditions among the elderly are uneven; although the majority live in adequate or comfortable circumstances, a large minority languish in poverty. A substantial number of old people own their own homes and seem to cherish the independence this brings them, while others reside in life-care communities, congregate living arrangements, or nursing homes; and still others reside in run-down city hotels, or depressed rural areas.

Although the statistical information provided by this chapter is essential in forming a general picture of the elderly, it tells us very little about the experience of being old—the joys and sorrows, attitudes toward life, perspectives on the past, or the self-image of an older person. To fill in these details, which vary widely among individuals, we must begin looking at some individual lives.

Maggie Kuhn,
founder of the
Gray Panthers

CHAPTER THREE

THE
AGELESS ONES

Throughout history, almost every age has been distinguished by a handful of old people who have stood out because of their remarkable achievements. In recent years, these individuals have grown substantially in number, as the elderly population increased. We might call such people The Ageless Ones, for their lives and their talents seem almost untouched by the hands of time.

In a study conducted a few decades ago, researchers discovered that some human beings experience two periods of intense creativity. These periods are the early years of adulthood and old age. For instance, some of the world's most famous poems were written by people aged twenty-five to twenty-nine and aged eighty to eighty-four. Seventy well-known authors produced their greatest works in their thirties and early forties, as well as in their sixties. And a large number of renowned artists enjoyed great bursts of creativity during their thirties and again in their seventies.

Michelangelo, for example, was busily painting the Sistine Chapel right up until he died at the age of eighty-nine. Artist Claude Monet created some of his most unusual works, the large murals of water lilies, during the seventh and eighth decades of his life. Grandma Moses didn't even begin her painting career until she was seventy-six, and she was still producing her primitive masterpieces at one hundred.

Many musicians have also continued performing successfully well into their advanced years. Pianist Artur Rubenstein remained an internationally acclaimed concert virtuoso into his nineties. And two Spaniards—the cellist Pablo Casals and the guitarist Andrés Segovia—were still performing to packed concert halls in their eighties.

Writers, too, have created some of their most enduring works in old age. It took Goethe more than sixty years before he finally completed his masterpiece *Faust* at the age of eighty-one. George Bernard Shaw had already reached his sixties when he published *St. Joan,* one of his most widely acclaimed plays. And the famous mystery writer Agatha Christie continued writing novels and plays at a furious pace into old age.

Among this century's best known political leaders, Charles De Gaulle became premier of France when he was already in his late sixties. De Gaulle then undertook the task of rescuing his country from a grave political crisis and restoring French prestige around the world. No doubt the greatest statesman of the modern era was Winston Churchill. In 1940, as Great Britain teetered on the brink of defeat at the hands of the Nazis, Churchill became

Mother Teresa, born in 1910, won the 1979 Nobel Peace Prize for her work among the poorest people of India.

prime minister. He was then sixty-five; and during the next five years he maintained a work schedule that would have killed many a younger man. During his country's darkest hours, he worked tirelessly to rally the British people. Eventually, the tide of war was reversed, and in the end total victory was secured. In 1945, Churchill left office, but his prodigious work schedule did not end. Between 1948 and 1953, he wrote a six-volume history of World War II, followed by the four-volume *A History of The English-Speaking Peoples*. Churchill's greatest achievements, the ones for which he is best remembered, all occurred when he had already become an old man.

As this brief discussion suggests, many people remain extremely active and make significant contributions to society during old age. Only a few of them make the history books; millions more are quiet, unsung "heroes" whose stories we never hear about.

The rest of this chapter will focus on four of The Ageless Ones. Two of them were world-famous; the other two are simply "average" people. Nevertheless, they seem to share many of the same characteristics, demonstrated repeatedly during the course of their lives, that appear to have influenced their old age.

SYMBOL OF AN AGE

No man better represents the spirit of our nation's early years than Benjamin Franklin. He was at once author, scientist, politician, statesman, American.

The music of composer Eubie Blake, born in 1883, inspired a Broadway musical, "Eubie." Blake wrote countless songs and played up to the time of his death in 1983.

Franklin's career began when he was apprenticed as a boy to his half-brother, James, a printer in Boston. After the two had a falling-out, Franklin left the city and traveled on his own to Philadelphia in search of employment. Early on, he demonstrated the independence of spirit which would characterize his entire life. In Philadelphia, Franklin eventually became owner and publisher of *The Pennsylvania Gazette,* one of the American colonies' foremost newspapers. As biographer Ronald Clark put it, Franklin's accomplishments as a newspaper publisher were due to a single-mindedness of purpose—a desire to achieve, to be successful—that would mark so many of his undertakings.

But it was not the *Gazette* that would be Franklin's enduring legacy in the publishing world, it was *Poor Richard's Almanack.* As Franklin described it:

> *Lunations . . . Eclipsses, Planets, Motions and Aspects. Weather, Sun and Moon's rising and setting. Highwater . . . besides many pleasant and witty Verses, Jests and sayings . . . by Richard Saunders Philomat.*

The *Almanack* sold 10,000 copies annually, making it an enormous best-seller for the times.

Franklin's interests were not narrowly confined to printing, however. In 1727, he founded the Junto Club, which met weekly to discuss the most important issues of the day. Out of these discussions arose the first Public Library of Philadelphia. Franklin played an important role in establishing the University of Pennsylvania; and he founded the American Philosophical Society, whose mem-

Benjamin Franklin

bers throughout the colonies corresponded on topics ranging from economics to botany.

In the 1740s, Franklin—who had already achieved substantial financial success—decided to spend less time on business so he could devote more of himself to one of his enduring interests: science. As Clark has pointed out, it was Franklin's skepticism, his questioning nature, and his willingness to innovate that made him such an effective scientist. Franklin investigated the origin of storms along the Atlantic seaboard; he invented the so-called "Franklin" stove; and he even speculated on the earth's history.

> *It is evident from the quantities of seashells, and the bones and teeth of fishes found in high land, that the sea has formerly covered them. Then, either the sea has been higher than it is now, and has fallen away from those high lands; or they have been lower than they are, and were lifted up. . . .*

· But it was Franklin's theory that lightning is a form of electricity which secured for all time his scientific reputation. His friend, the British chemist Joseph Priestley, described the well-known experiment used to prove the theory, as Franklin related it to him.

> *The kite being raised, a considerable time elapsed before there was any appearance of its being electrified . . . he [Franklin] immediately presented his knuckle to the key and . . . the discovery was complete. He perceived a very evident electric spark.*

For his discovery, Franklin was elected to the British Royal Society and the French Academy of Science—the first American ever to receive such honors.

In 1757, when Franklin sailed to England to serve as a colonial agent, his fame preceded him. His career as a statesman had begun, a career that would consume the remainder of his lifetime. Except for a brief period in the 1760s, Franklin remained in England until 1775, working tirelessly to avoid war. As his friend Joseph Priestley wrote, Franklin "took every method in his power to prevent a rupture between the two countries. He dreaded the war and often said that if the difference should come to an open rupture, it would be a war of ten years, and he should not live to see the end of it." Franklin would be mistaken, of course, on both counts.

As war loomed, Franklin left England and sailed for home. He had now reached the advanced age of seventy, but this did not prevent him from composing, during the course of the voyage, 250 pages describing his recent negotiations with the British. He also took time to pursue one of his enduring interests, a study of the Gulf Stream. Franklin conducted experiments on its temperature and depth so he could accurately describe the Gulf Stream to the world.

Benjamin Franklin would remain in America barely long enough to serve as a delegate to the Continental Congress and help draft the Declaration of Independence. He then returned to Europe for his most important diplomatic mission, ambassador to France. Here was an old, overweight American, plagued by gout as well as various other illnesses, who nevertheless became the darling of French society and a great hero to the entire nation. During his years as ambassador, Franklin played a crucial role in forging the American alliance with France, an alliance which virtually assured independence.

Franklin was not entirely occupied with diplomatic issues, however. He took time to write part of his autobiography, attended meetings of the French Academy of Science, and even observed the beginnings of ballooning. Of manned balloon flights, he wrote: "Convincing sovereigns of the folly of wars may perhaps be one effect of it, since it will be impracticable for the most potent of them to guard their dominions."

On his return voyage from France in 1785, Franklin, now eighty, continued his observations of the Gulf Stream. He also wrote three papers: one on the Gulf Stream and other maritime subjects, a second on how to prevent smoking chimneys, and a third on methods of improving coal-burning stoves.

In 1787, Franklin attended the Constitutional Convention where he played a major role in bringing about the Great Compromise which led to the adoption of the U.S. Constitution. As Franklin neared the end of his long career and active participation in the great events of his country, an observer could still describe him this way:

He has an incessant vein of humor, accompanied with an uncommon vivacity, which seems as natural and involuntary as his breathing.

Franklin's energy, his enthusiasm, his sense of humor, and his wide-ranging interests were vitally important in making not only his old age but his entire life rich and productive. He was possessed of an enormous desire to succeed at whatever he undertook. And he seems never to have lost that unquenchable curiosity that characterizes any gifted inventor or statesman, or for that matter, any human being who remains vitally involved with the affairs of life.

CITIZEN OF THE WORLD

Margaret Mead once called her grandmother "the most decisive influence in my life." Her grandmother had become a high school principal in an era when very few women ever dared to pursue careers. (Mead's mother held a Ph.D. degree, an achievement also quite rare for a woman around the turn of the century.) Thus Margaret grew up in a family who demonstrated that a woman could be the equal of any man, quite a revolutionary idea for the early twentieth century. They also instilled in young Margaret an inner-directedness: the confidence to trust in herself, chart her own course, and not be shackled by conventions or the opinions of others. This inner-directedness fueled a unique brand of involvement with people and events that would continue throughout her lifetime.

Margaret Mead began pursuing an independent course early. At twenty-three, she was a disciple of famed anthropologist Franz Boas. As part of their training, Boas sent his students out into the field to live with native cultural groups so they could gain firsthand experience of their customs. He had decided to send Margaret to a North American Indian tribe where she was to study adolescents and determine whether they were subject to the same stress as adolescents growing up in our culture. But Margaret insisted that she should go instead to someplace more exotic, like the South Seas, and Boas finally relented. Thus, a young woman who had never traveled out of the country —let alone into a primitive culture—embarked on a long, tiring journey to Samoa in 1925.

Out of Mead's experiences and observations, came the first of her many books, *Coming of Age in Samoa*. In it, she pointed out that cultural differences between the United States and the Samoan tribes produced very different patterns of growing up. An adolescent's emotional turmoil and rebellion, in other words, were not inherent. It was not only the book's conclusions that seemed remarkable (nor the fact that it was written by a woman), but its clear, simple style could be read and understood by the general public. As a result, the book—and its author—became widely known.

Mead made subsequent expeditions and wrote more books—*Growing Up in New Guinea* and *Sex and Temperament in Three Primitive Societies*. Through her travels, Margaret Mead developed an empathy and respect for the values of every society. She could overcome cultural barriers and find the common threads that united all humanity in a way that truly made her a citizen of the world.

So many of the same issues that concerned the world's people seemed to interest her too: education, ecology, women's rights, nuclear war, and, especially, the family. Mead recognized that the family was one of society's most enduring institutions because of its essential role in raising and instilling cultural values in children, that is socializing them. Nevertheless, she was often harshly critical of the isolated nuclear family, and lamented the fact that grandparents no longer played a vital role in family living. In her book, *Family*, published when Mead was already in her sixties, she wrote:

> *From grandparents, children learn about the whole cycle of life—what it is like to have grown children, to have lived a full life, to have completed the tasks one has set for oneself, and to grow old. Old age seen only from a distance can be frightening. . . . But children can be rescued from a fear of old people by the presence of just one loved grandparent, great-aunt, or grandparent of a friend who is companionable with the very young.*

Margaret Mead had learned the truth of these words from her own grandmother. To her, old age was not to be feared because it formed part of the seamless fabric of life.

Her own old age was living proof that a long life could still be full and rewarding. According to one of her biographers, Mead routinely began her day reading or writing at 5:00 A.M. Later she would teach courses and meet with students, and in the evening appear for one of the many speaking engagements that filled her calendar. I once heard her speak in Washington, D.C. She walked to the

*Margaret Mead holding
her thumbstick*

podium with the aid of the thumbstick (or cane) that had become her trademark. Mead was famous for her strong spirit; she rarely shrank from taking an unpopular position on an issue or roundly criticizing others if they didn't agree with her. This time her subject was sex education in the schools, something she had supported for years because she believed it would help develop more fulfilling marriage relationships. Mead often spoke for an hour without any notes. That way, she said, she could never give the same speech twice, which would bore her.

In addition to her speaking engagements, Mead also wrote a monthly column for *Redbook* magazine from 1961 until her death in 1978. The column offered advice to women on a variety of topics, including birth control, marriage, and child rearing. It is probably not surprising that Mead was one of the early advocates of equal rights for women. But she never embraced the positions of some of her more radical sisters who demeaned the role of housewife and mother, or blamed all women's problems on men.

In 1970, at the age of sixty-nine, Mead wrote a book on another issue of great concern to her—relations between the generations. Titled *Culture and Commitment: A Study of The Generation Gap*, it pointed out that today's generation gap had opened partly because children were currently living through events that their parents had never experienced: space travel, computer technology, and nuclear war. Parents were simply unequipped to teach their children about these things; they had to learn about them on their own. But Mead had long believed that one way of bridging the gap was through grandparents. As she had earlier written:

> . . . *contemporary grandparents . . . carry out their age-old function of teaching their grandchildren how the whole of life is lived to its conclusion—in the past by running exactly the same course that one's father had run, and today by a readiness to run each day, each week, each year a new and untried course.*

Margaret Mead herself exemplified this philosophy throughout her life. She seemed to thrive on newness and change, to possess that persistent desire to explore and experiment, to be at the center of the action or—as she once put it—in the eye of the hurricane. And even in her final year, when she was losing her battle with cancer, Mead continued her extremely busy schedule.

Few of us may ever reach the prominence of Margaret Mead or possess the energy to carry on so full a life. Nevertheless, we can take comfort from knowing that old age need not be a time to retire or cut short our activities. There are still too many things to do, too many people who need us, too many reasons to remain involved with life.

ONE ON ONE

I interviewed Sheila in the living room of her tiny home just off the coast of Florida. Sheila is not world-famous like Margaret Mead, but she does possess some of the same qualities, among them an indomitable spirit which refuses to let old age get the better of her. Sheila refused to tell me how old she was. I suspect she had, at the very least, reached her late seventies. Although she lived in Florida, an area renowned for its old-age homes and retirement communities, Sheila was hardly living in retirement.

Sheila told me that her entire career had been spent in the entertainment field, either on the stage or on the radio. She had first entered the theater while still a girl, over the very strong objections of her parents. As a result, she couldn't count on them for any financial support and had to work part time to pay for her training.

"I was very determined. I was very stubborn," Sheila explained in her rich British-accented voice.

She recalled that one day the famed Shakespearean actress Ellen Terry caught one of her performances in acting class. "My child, you have talent," Terry told her. "You should be on the stage." It was all the encouragement Sheila needed.

Sheila acted on stage for about eight years, appearing at the Old Vic and performing in such plays as *The Beggar's Opera*. While playing in *Paradise Lost*, she had been seen by a member of the Board of Governors of the British Broadcasting Company (BBC), who asked her to come in for an audition. To work for the BBC in those days, Sheila said, you had to speak two foreign languages fluently, possess a working knowledge of music and drama, and—because it was hard to record women's voices without making them sound squeaky—have a deep voice. She got the job.

Sheila began working for the BBC about 1930, doing radio plays. For these presentations, a group of people would stand around a microphone, and, with very little other than their voices, recreate all the drama of a theatrical performance. In 1933, Sheila became a permanent member of the BBC staff, which meant she had other broadcasting assignments, including reading the news. She was the first woman ever to do so.

"The public hated me reading the news," Sheila recalled. "They wrote in by the dozens saying 'take this woman away. We don't want to hear the news from her. We don't believe a word she says.'"

The BBC bowed to public opinion and took Sheila off the news. But she continued with her other assignments, which included the radio plays as well as announcing concerts and variety shows. At this time she was the only woman announcer on the BBC and about the only one anywhere in the world. Sheila explained, "I love the challenge of doing radio . . . and the peace and quiet. I've always been rather a one on one person and that's why I love radio. It's the only medium left where [it's] just you and the microphone."

The most rewarding thing she ever did, Sheila told me, was broadcasting to the British troops during World War II. By that time there were other women broadcasters; they announced music programs and theater performances and also answered the many love letters written to them by the men at the front. After the war Sheila introduced a new radio program called "Spotlight on Women", on which she interviewed well-known women and also invited men to come on the air for "equal time." One of her most memorable guests was Winston Churchill.

In the 1950s, when her husband decided to move to the United States and into semiretirement, Sheila came with him. She worked for two radio stations, both of which went out of business. She then became involved with a fund-raising effort to put an FM "good music station" on the air, but that didn't succeed either. "I was so depressed," Sheila recalled. "I said I would never go through that again."

Then she received a call from a listener who suggested that there were many people in the area who would support a classical music station. Sheila promptly sent out 1,000 letters and received over 300 replies. Sometime later she spotted an advertisement in the paper saying that a local FM station was looking for new program ideas. "So I went over and sold them on this one," Sheila said.

She's had her own show ever since. It was a classic case of not giving up and admitting defeat, even when the odds were against her.

Today, Sheila does three one-hour radio programs and a thirty-minute television show every week. Each of the presentations takes about five hours of preparation. "This is called retiring," Sheila says.

A typical program might include a review of a concert, followed by an interview with some of the musicians. "You decide on a line that would bring the person out," she explained. "The important thing is to make them feel absolutely at home and happy . . . [then] hope that they don't dry up on you."

Sheila recalled one unsettling experience when someone did "dry up"—an actor who was appearing in a local theater performance.

He came to be interviewed and to all my questions he either said "yes" or "no" or "I don't remember." And the fifteen-minute sign came up [meaning fifteen minutes left to go in her TV program] *and I realized I didn't have another question left. And I remember sitting thinking: I wonder what people do when this happens. And I suddenly remembered that someone had told me that he was interested in vitamins. So I said, "I understand you're interested in vitamins." He lit up like a Christmas tree and talked for fifteen minutes.*

One of the things she enjoys most about her work, Sheila explained, is that each show is different. The variety keeps her from getting bored. But it's more than just the variety; it's her commitment to doing something meaningful, something that is deeply appreciated by many others. "People like my programs," Sheila said, "and they come up and tell me so."

Her husband having died some years ago, Sheila lives alone now, except for her cat. But a cat isn't enough to drive away the loneliness of an empty house. This is one of the burdens of growing old that Sheila just has to live with.

"There's nothing good about old age," she states emphatically. But she refuses to give in to it.

Sheila possesses a resolute spirit that has sustained her throughout an entire lifetime—from her initial decision to enter the theater over the objections of her parents to her refusal to give up until she finally had her own radio and television shows in the United States. Now in old age she remains much too independent to accept the prevailing view that old people should simply retire and stay home. Sheila continues to be active. She grows impatient with boring routine and continually seeks the new and different. And she is still engaged in the same love affair with the arts that she has pursued since childhood.

THE WRITER

"I had known since the sixth grade that I wanted to be in journalism."

Bob has been a professional writer and journalist for over forty-five years. When I first met him, and throughout the interviews that followed, I was struck by how much he seemed to resemble the person I might be (or hoped I might be) in my old age.

By the time he had graduated from college, Bob realized that he "didn't want to be a reporter who was out on a different kind of an assignment every day and wound up knowing something about everything but no one subject in depth."

Bob wanted to specialize in one particular area, to become an "authority," as he put it. He explained that there were three areas of business that looked very appealing in the 1930s when he was finishing college: radio broadcasting, air conditioning, and aviation. Bob decided on aviation and before long he succeeded in landing a job with a magazine in Washington, D.C.

Bob explained that being involved in aviation constantly gave him a chance to learn new things, because the field was constantly changing. "It was very exciting, still is," Bob said, in his clipped midwestern accent. As chief editor for the magazine, he once scooped every other publication in the country by publishing an account of the first airplane to break the sound barrier. Later, Bob was involved in setting up a new aviation magazine, given the assignment (by the owner) of creating something that would be indispensable to the entire industry. This magazine got the reputation for "telling it like it is," Bob recalled, "even if the executives of a particular airline didn't always like what they read."

This spirit of independence finally led Bob to clash with his boss over the issue of editorial freedom (Bob's freedom to publish what he thought was right). He resigned from the magazine, and later went to work as public relations chief for a large aircraft company. But after only a brief stint, Bob returned once again to his first love, aviation publishing. During these years in journalism, he also found time to meet his future wife, who worked for a brief period as his secretary. Bob recalled fondly how wonderful it was to come home each evening and discuss the day's events with someone who understood precisely what he had experienced.

Eventually Bob found himself in a job that was phased out because of budgetary cutbacks, and he was forced to take early retirement. In many ways, Bob said, retirement provided a welcome change because it gave him the freedom to do things on his own. The question Bob now had to answer was exactly what he wanted to do. He still wished to remain as active as possible, and he needed to earn some money, so he began writing letters to anyone he could think of, looking for work. Bob compares the process to throwing pebbles into a pond and watching to see what happens. Apparently one of these pebbles attracted some attention, because he got a call from the editor of a local newspaper offering him a full-time job. But Bob declined the offer.

"When you are facing freedom for the first time," he explained, "you don't want to tie yourself up immediately when all these other things are beckoning to you—even though you don't know exactly what they are."

Throughout his life, Bob had never been frightened off by the unknown; more than once he left a job he didn't want to support his family by freelancing. And this was to be no exception. Eventually he did join the staff of that local newspaper part time, as one of its editors. He also works for a small publishing company putting together book deals on town histories and other topics. Recently, Bob finished a market research project for a friend who runs a small airline. Still, he doesn't believe his life is quite full enough. "I have a little extra time, and I'm trying to decide what to do with it," Bob said, "what area offers some promise."

Bob has an infectious enthusiasm for life and an interest in events that comes, perhaps, from his years as a journalist—probing, asking questions, and searching for answers. As Bob put it:

> *Every day that I read about the real world, I can't imagine why people read fiction. It's exciting. Every day . . . you wonder what you're going to hit next. If you're interested in learning . . . and delving into the whys and wherefores, and if you're trying to forecast what is going to happen next—which I was always trying to do—it's pretty exciting.*

The Ageless Ones are people who exemplify certain attitudes, developed throughout a lifetime, that seem to affect the quality of their old age. One of these is an independent spirit—a willingness to stand out from the crowd, to be different. This type of attitude may be important for all of us if we hope to escape the stereotype of old age as a period of retirement or inactivity, and to make it instead a time for active involvement. The Ageless Ones also seem to have a variety of interests which they pursue over the entire course of their lives. These are people who never seem content to rest or do nothing, but are always looking for another challenge. As Bob explained, old age is "quite rewarding for someone who has an active mind." These are indeed minds that are flexible, willing to experiment, to change. Inflexible people often get left behind, or put out to pasture, where they are quite easily forgotten. By contrast, the Ageless Ones have an indomitability that keeps them going even in the face of adversity, whether they're trying to get their own radio program, like Sheila, or they're phased out of a job and forced to find new work, like Bob.

Finally, these individuals seem to possess a commitment to something greater than themselves—whether it was Franklin's commitment to the future of his country, or Mead's to the future of our world; Bob's commitment to journalism, or Sheila's to the performing arts. As Sheila put it, you need a "reason to get up in the morning."

The Ageless Ones possess these reasons in great abundance.

CHAPTER FOUR

THE REALITY
OF
RETIREMENT

For millions of working Americans, retirement marks the passage into old age. Like other important events such as a twenty-first birthday or a marriage, retirement often occasions an elaborate celebration featuring a special dinner, the presentation of a gold watch or other gift to the retiree, and many thanks for a job well done. But all the fine speeches and polite applause can't cover up the fact that the retiree doesn't have that job any longer; it now belongs to a younger person.

As we saw in the last chapter, the Ageless Ones avoided retirement altogether. We should consider ourselves extremely fortunate that the concept of retirement was virtually unknown in Franklin's time—he would have been considered too old to become a Founding Father. We are equally fortunate that Margaret Mead simply decided to ignore the entire notion. As for Sheila and Bob, they also refused to retire and found ways to keep on working.

But the overwhelming majority of Americans do retire. Some adjust very poorly. Many others, however, adjust much more successfully. Experts point to a few significant factors that seem to affect the quality of an individual's retirement. One of these is money—that is, an income sufficient to ensure economic security. Another factor seems to be a fulfilling family relationship, a subject we will look at more closely in the next chapter. Third, good physical health plays a vital role in a satisfying retirement, as we will see in Chapter Six. Finally, a positive mental attitude distinguishes successful retirees. They approach life in the same way as the Ageless Ones, involving themselves in a full range of meaningful activities.

This chapter will focus on the attitudes of retirees by examining a full range of retirement experiences and drawing some conclusions from them that may be useful to the rest of us.

WHAT DOES RETIREMENT MEAN?

To some, retirement stand for old age in all its negative aspects. Ours is a society where individuals largely define their identities by the type of jobs they have. Simply stated, we are what we do. By contrast, the word "retirement" implies doing nothing. So the retiree can easily feel like someone who has suddenly lost all identity.

Under these circumstances, it isn't surprising that some people who fully realize retirement is fast approaching may still try to deny it. "I won't have to retire," these people might say, "I'm much too valuable. How will the company run without me?" These individuals will probably refuse to participate in their company's pre-retirement program, where issues such as retirement income, health benefits, and legal and tax questions are discussed.

As retirement draws closer and the reality of it becomes inescapable, these individuals may begin to feel angry. "Why do I have to retire?" they might say. "No one can do this job any better than I can. It's just not fair!" These fits of anger may alternate with feelings of depression over all the changes retirement will surely bring. As one man explained to me: "Everyone says retirement will be terrific. But it's not the same. I don't feel involved . . . no one is demanding anything of me. I need something that is demanded of me."

Retirement brings an abrupt end to a daily routine that for many people has lasted for forty years or more. No doubt they were heard to complain from time to time about the "rat race," with its unrelenting pressure, or the boss and his impossible deadlines. But most people also like to experience the sense of accomplishment that comes from having something "demanded" of them and doing it successfully. Retirement changes all of this: nothing is demanded because you aren't expected to do anything.

For some, it's not the job that means so much to them, but the people. Individuals look forward to seeing their co-workers, doing projects together, and socializing on the job or at the end of the day. Retirement severs these connections, reducing the opportunities for socializing, and often leaving people feeling alone and adrift.

The onset of retirement also produces a significant drop in income for most people. Of course, expenses for such items as clothing and transportation may decline too, but other costs, like heating fuel, medical care, and real estate taxes, will continue to rise. So retirees often have good reason to worry about whether they'll have enough money to make ends meet.

Perhaps all these factors account for the results of a recent poll of retirees in which one-half of them said that they would prefer to be working, at least part time. The American Medical Association has pointed to another reason why meaningful activities such as part-time work are extremely important. As the AMA put it, a "direct relationship exists between enforced idleness and poor health." This statement applies to everyone, young or old. All of us need something meaningful to do to preserve our physical and psychological well-being. Although medical science has made it possible for more and more people to reach old age, the important question is not how long will we live, but what will the quality of our lives be. Today, an increasing number of options are becoming available that can make the quality of retirement and old age better than ever.

PHASED RETIREMENT

To reduce the shock people feel when they're working full time one week and find themselves out of work the next, some companies have instituted phased retirement programs. As workers near the time to retire, they can gradually reduce their work load to four days a week or even less. Job sharing is a new idea. An older woman, for example, shares her job with a young mother who needs time away from work to care for her child. One company even grants workers a paid leave of absence to give them an opportunity to explore new interests and develop different life-styles in preparation for their retirement.

Evelyn Smith serves as co-director of a retiree's job bank at the Traveler's Insurance Company in Hartford, Connecticut. Ms. Smith had taken early retirement from Traveler's some time ago; but after only about a year, she began looking around for something "more constructive to do with my life." At first, she worked for a temporary employment agency helping older people find jobs. Then Traveler's started its job-bank program and asked her to come back and help run it.

During a preretirement planning session, Ms. Smith explained, employees are given the opportunity of adding their names to the job bank. So far, about 200 out of a possible 2,500 employees in Connecticut have signed up, making them eligible for temporary assignments at Traveler's. An opening may occur in the same area where the retiree worked, but the person might also help out in a different department. Today, retirees hold temporary positions as secretaries, clerks, systems analysts, and underwriters. And the cost to Traveler's is less than going outside and hiring people through a temporary employment agency.

Many other companies have used similar approaches, keeping older people on the payroll to take advantage of their experience. Of course, these companies have been forced to do some tinkering with their pension programs which have very strict rules governing when and under what circumstances a worker can begin receiving benefits. Traveler's Insurance Company, for example, now allows its retirees to work up to 960 hours annually without forfeiting any benefits. At other companies, older people who exceed a certain number of part-time hours must wait to start receiving their pensions; but they can apply these hours to receive even larger benefits when they "retire" a second time.

John Toppin, vice-president of human resources for a company in western Massachusetts, has instituted an imaginative preretirement program that emphasizes public service. The program permits older employees to gradually replace the number of days they work for the company with volunteer work in the community. Employees select the organization where they want to volunteer, and make the transition during their last year before retirement, while continuing to receive full pay. One person works for the Council on Aging; another waits on tables in the coffee shop of a nearby hospital; a third teaches drafting, algebra, and trigonometry at a local high school. Toppin agrees that the program is "not appropriate for everyone." And only a few preretirees have signed up for it so far. But, as Toppin explains, it does provide an "opportunity to phase into something," and it's meaningful not only for the retiree but for the community as well.

A LIFE OF LEISURE

The majority of older people neither participate in phased retirement programs nor undertake part-time employment. Many seem ready, even eager, to simply retire and enjoy the life of leisure that they have dreamed about for so long. How do they spend all these leisure hours?

Studies show that some old people spend more time watching television, gardening, or "just doing nothing." A number of factors may explain why they seem to prefer staying at home engaged in largely sedentary activities. An older person's declining vigor and health would dictate more sedentary pursuits; while a reduced income would make homebound activities most easily affordable. Another, more subtle explanation may be that old people believe the role of an aged, retired individual should simply be to sit around, doing as little as possible. After all, isn't that what our society seems to expect? Unfortunately, this leaves old people with an extremely limited set of options. Having few activities to occupy their time, and confining themselves to a solitary life-style, the elderly may be sadly disappointed with the life of leisure that they anticipated for so many years.

Fortunately, many old people succeed in avoiding this potentially harmful situation. Some regularly attend senior citizens' centers; these are found in large and small communities in every region of the country. The center in my community offers transportation for those who are unable to drive, as well as lunch five days a week. A variety of services are also available, including income tax advice, legal assistance, and health screening. But senior citizens' centers are probably best known for the wide array of leisure activities they provide, and mine is no exception. Each week boasts a full calendar of events, featuring physical fitness, bingo, dancing, cake decorating, macramé, tennis, rug hooking, movies, and bridge. The elderly can also enroll in academic courses leading to a high school diploma. Many old people arrive by 10:00 A.M., when the activities begin, and remain until mid-afternoon when the buses leave to take them home.

Two friends shooting
a game of pool

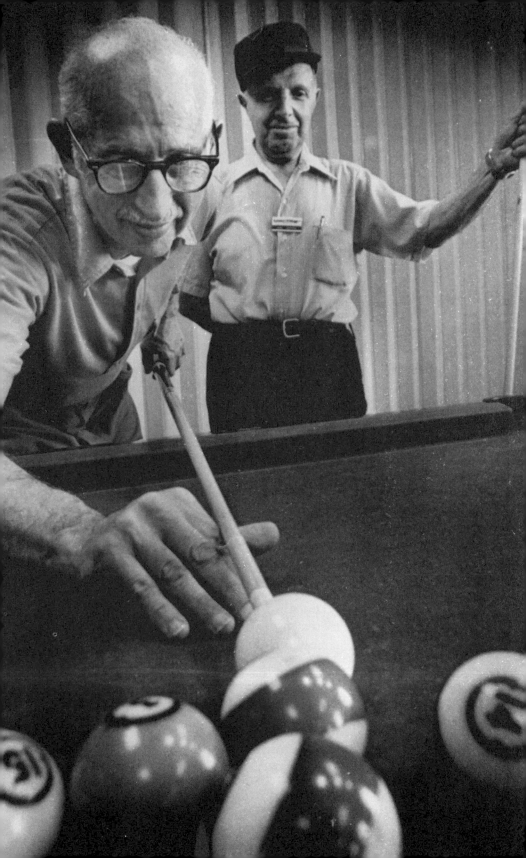

For a number of months, I attended a program at the center called "Living History." Each week an old person would address the group and recount his or her experiences while growing up. The recollections were taped as a resource for the local schools to provide a continuing link with the past. As the director of the program explained, most young people can't get this kind of information directly because they either don't have grandparents or don't see them very often.

One man remembered getting up at 4:00 every morning to load a milk truck and help with deliveries, for which he received the princely sum of 25 cents an hour. Then he hopped a trolley and put in a full day at school. A woman fondly recalled one of her teachers who "instilled in me a love of literature" and "got me to write the class hymn." Others described football games, picnics, and proms. But all agreed that school rules were quite different when they were young. Boys were strapped for misbehaving. Smoking was absolutely forbidden. And girls with the audacity to wear lipstick were sent promptly to the principal who wiped it off.

While attending the Living History program, I met Ernie, a man possessed of an indomitable spirit. Ernie once told me that he had successfully gotten rid of his arthritis by simply not giving in to it and continuing to exercise. "I'm the captain of my body," he said more than once. But later, Ernie had been stricken by a debilitating stroke from which he had never fully recovered.

Ernie has three children and he traveled between them, spending about four months of the year with each one. Before his retirement, Ernie had pursued a long, active career as an engineer, continuing to work well into his seventies.

"Life's no bed of roses," Ernie said. "But you can't give up. Too many people give up." As I rose to leave, Ernie shook my hand. I felt a grip still firm and sure. Ernie was not giving up no matter what happened.

VOLUNTEER PROGRAMS

As volunteers, old people represent an extremely valuable human resource, and throughout the country they are donating their time and energies to many different activities. A number are involved in environmental groups. Some have carried on a life-long interest in the environment; for others, the involvement began only after retirement. One woman helps care for wounded birds at an animal hospital in her local Audubon society. A retired accountant works in a nearby office of Friends of the Earth doing bookkeeping and correspondence; while a retired tool-and-die maker leads hikes and biking trips for nature enthusiasts. Under a program sponsored by the National Park Service, elderly people can also become volunteer rangers, leading tours for visitors at national monuments.

In Santa Ana, California, a project known as PACE (Psychological Alternative Counseling for Elders) has enlisted the aid of old people to act as peer counselors. The elderly attend a nine-week training program in which they learn how to recognize the problems of other aged individuals and offer support. To be effective counselors, elderly trainees must be understanding and empathetic, nonjudgmental, and willing to help without trying to impose their own solutions on others. Peer counselors travel to senior citizens' centers or to clients' homes providing support for old people who are coping with such problems as the loss of a spouse, a long illness, or the problems of living on a fixed income.

A variety of volunteer programs for the elderly are sponsored by the government. The Small Business Administration funds SCORE (Service Corps of Retired Executives) which offers advice to small businesses. The Administration on Aging initiated RSVP (Retired Senior Volunteer Program) through which volunteers sixty or older can donate their time in parks, museums, day care centers, hospitals, and libraries. Foster Grandparents, another program, matches older people who are at or below the poverty level with handicapped children in families or institutions. The old people receive a small stipend for their work. But the real value, not only for them but for the children, comes from the warm, satisfying relationships that develop. Senior Companion Program (SCP) is similar to Foster Grandparents except that the recipients are older persons instead of children.

A NEW LIFE

Experts point out that old people are often faced with the need to create new identities for themselves after retirement. The elderly no longer work full time, so they can't use their jobs to define who they are. They are also unlikely to be full-time parents or homemakers, so they can't continue to identify with these roles either. The realization they must change produces feelings of anxiety and confusion for old people, as it does for any of us. But change may be more difficult for the old because their habits are much more ingrained. Nevertheless, many old people seem willing to take risks and strike out in different directions in order to create new roles for themselves.

A few years ago, Marie suddenly found herself alone, with plenty of time on her hands and not much to do with it. Her husband had just died; her children had already grown up and moved away. Marie's story could fit millions of older women today, but not all of them deal with it so effectively. Marie became involved in a program called Elderhostel. Through Elderhostel, older people live for a week or two on college campuses—in the United States and abroad—while they are enrolled in minicourses.

"I felt self-conscious about taking courses," Marie admitted. "I had only a two-year degree and thought I would be out of place. But I loved it." Marie had always maintained a special interest in writing, so as her first course she chose "How to Write Children's Books." Marie contributed an article to the magazine *Expanding Horizons* that students produced as part of the course. The success

*A foster grandmother with
her two foster grandchildren*

she achieved in the Elderhostel Program encouraged her to continue writing. Other articles followed. Later came a book of poetry and lyrics, followed by another book of poetry and short stories. Marie published the books privately and handled the sales herself. It wasn't easy.

"You have to be gutsy," Marie explained with a laugh. "I went into [my local] bookstore and asked them if they would put it [my first book] on the shelf, and they took ten on consignment. The manager put it right by the cash register. She sold forty for me," Marie recalled enthusiastically. "So I brought in my next book of poems and she sold fifty of those. Then they gave me an autograph party."

Here is an excerpt from Marie's books of poems and lyrics:

Le Wig

When Old Father Time
has caused your hair
to fall
like the leaves
in Autumn,
'tis time to resort
to that great invention
the one, the only—
Le Wig!
The possibilities
are endless
be bold
be a blonde
brunette or
red head—
depending on your mood
and if you're
truly daring—

why not
a different shade
each week??

PREPARATION
FOR A LIFETIME

"I don't have time to worry about retirement. I'll start thinking about that when I'm in my sixties."

These are the words of a young, hard-working professional friend of mine. His approach is fairly typical of most adults. Yet job experts point out that you should begin thinking about retirement long before your sixties—and even preparing for it.

Of course, most people realize that they should save some money for retirement, so they'll have sufficient funds to supplement their social security checks. But preparation involves much more. It means developing positive mental attitudes to sustain you today, tomorrow, and into your retirement years, for these years may comprise up to one-third of your life.

Create a life-style for yourself which is not completely focused on a job by developing leisure interests which you can pursue for a lifetime. One man I knew quite well was a jazz buff during most of his life. He also played tennis regularly and could still carry on a vigorous game of doubles into his seventies. Moreover, for many years, he had operated his own short-wave radio station, communicating nightly with other operators all over the world. And, as if this weren't enough to keep him occupied, he contributed a weekly word puzzle to his local newspaper.

Martin, a tall, heavy-set man, spent most of his life as a house painter and decorator until his retirement. Through most of his life he maintained an interest in wood carving. As a teenager, Martin recalled, he taught groups of youngsters how to carve and paint birds. Later, he had taken time out from his work to carve an eagle for the local fire station. And, when his community celebrated its 300th birthday, Martin donated his time to letter plaques to be hung on the front of historic houses.

After retirement, Martin continued his interest in carving and decorative painting by teaching these skills at a nearby senior citizens' center. Martin could take old people with little or no prior training and, as if by magic, have them producing beautiful wooden bird replicas in only a few weeks. Martin explained that, as a painter, he had taught his assistants how to hang wallpaper and mix colors. And this experience proved very useful to him when he instructed at the senior center.

When you taught them [his assistants], *in the back of your mind you would say: How did it happen? What's the best way to teach these people? And it all came back to me. Well, you've got to have patience . . . a lot of patience. It's fascinating to see someone turn out a piece that's real nice and you know you helped.*

Martin said that it hadn't been difficult for him to adjust to retirement. He had his carving, as well as a garden to tend, and from time to time he and his wife take trips together. The real problem, Martin explained, is that "I don't have enough time right now." He simply has too many things he wants to do.

One of the most important factors in a fulfilling retirement is the way each individual approaches it. People who have spent most of their lives thinking about little else besides their jobs and who believe that retirement signals an end to their usefulness will quite likely sit in a rocking chair and do nothing.

But those who have always pursued a variety of interests will discover that retirement only offers more time to enjoy them. And still others who are willing to begin something new—whether they volunteer to work in a community organization, enroll in an education program, or undertake a different career—will find that they are perfectly capable of succeeding at it. These individuals will continue to lead productive and satisfying lives.

*Two craftsmen continue working
at their craft into retirement.*

Through the miracles of medical science, most of us can look forward with confidence to long retirements. So we must decide whether to waste those years or utilize them effectively. It's not an exaggeration to say that we can begin preparing for retirement almost immediately by developing positive attitudes and broad, deep interests that can sustain and enrich us for a lifetime.

CHAPTER FIVE

THE AGED
AND THEIR
FAMILIES

A balding, paunchy executive, a few months into his retirement, sits across the kitchen table from his irate wife who acidly proclaims: "I may have married you for better or for worse, Howard, but not for lunch."

This story characterizes a widely held view of relationships between elderly husbands and wives. Without a full-time job to consume his energies, a retired man is necessarily condemned to spending his days padding aimlessly around the house. For want of anything better to do, he decides to take over the cleaning chores, then the grocery shopping, and even tries his hand at cooking meals. This infuriates his long-suffering wife who feels that her husband has usurped control of the household, which has been exclusively her domain. Meanwhile the rest of their relationship has long since started showing severe cracks. After years of devoting most of their attentions to making ends meet and raising a family, the couple now find that as they look across the table, each of them sees a stranger. With all

A couple in their kitchen

this time on their hands, they have very little to talk about and even less that they enjoy doing together. She wants to go out to the movies; he'd rather stay at home watching a baseball game. Eventually, their relationship deteriorates past the point of no return, and they decide to call it quits, after forty years of marriage, and go their separate ways.

There can be little question that this stereotype certainly fits some elderly couples. After all, a number of them show up in the divorce courts every year. But, for the great majority, the picture appears quite different. Research has shown that the level of happiness enjoyed by married couples reaches its highest point at two different stages of marriage: before the children are born, and after they have grown and moved away from home. A recent survey of married couples fifty and over conducted by Consumer's Union confirms this research. Over 4,200 people responded to questionnaires. Of those responding, 87 percent said that they were happily married, and most of these respondents were still married to the same spouse.

A major reason why older couples report a high level of happiness, experts believe, is that they face fewer pressures. Generally, a man or woman of fifty-five, sixty, or older no longer worries very much about advancing a career (which has almost run its course) or earning enough money to support a family. With these concerns largely at an end, a couple can now devote far more time to each other's needs.

Couples responding to the Consumer's Union survey pointed to effective communication as a key factor in their happiness. Being open, honest, and considerate, they said, were essentials in a fulfilling relationship. Of course, a married couple cannot wait until they reach old age to develop elements of effective communication. They must maintain and strengthen them throughout the entire course of their marriage. As one husband in the Consumer's Union survey said: "Love in the mature years is much more a sharing operation with a learned process of giving on both sides—a little less exciting but surer and deeper."

Popular opinion has long held that after people reach old age they somehow lose all interest in sex, or the ability to carry on sexual relations, and exist happily in platonic relationships. According to the data collected by Consumer's Union, nothing could be further from the truth. Almost 80 percent of those responding stated that they currently engaged in sexual relations. While most wives reported that they were satisfied with the frequency of sex, about 40 percent of the husbands said that they would have enjoyed relations more often.

In addition to answering the questions, one respondent included this note pointing out the survey's immense social value:

> *I know younger readers will thank you . . . because it gives them hope for their own old age. Older readers will thank you for bringing their feelings and actions out of the closet of inhibition and perhaps help them have joy in their old age.*

For years, experts have written about the so-called "empty nest" syndrome that afflicts women in middle and old age. Once their children grow up and leave the nest, these women feel that their lives no longer have any purpose, and nothing worthwhile remains for them to do. While some women must surely suffer from this problem, it did not characterize the majority who responded to the Consumer's Union survey. As one woman put it, "Now that the children are . . . gone, we are delighted to be a 'single couple' once again."

Far from having little to do, an increasing number of women must cope with the demands of full-time or part-time jobs. And, since a woman is generally younger than her husband, she may continue working even after he retires. Instead of a wife complaining that she doesn't want her husband home for lunch, he may find himself eating it alone.

This new role may take some getting-used-to. It is very easy for a husband to feel inadequate, watching his wife go off to work and bring in the pay check, when he always carried the honors as the family's primary breadwinner. Gerontologists suggest that married couples discuss these issues before retirement so they can work out methods of dealing with them successfully. One effective approach might be for a man to develop new interests that can sustain him after retirement, and to broaden his circle of friendships so he does not depend entirely on his wife for companionship.

BETWEEN PARENTS
AND CHILD

It is part of American folklore that in our golden past many families consisted of three generations—children, parents, and grandparents—living together under one roof. In fact, very few of these families ever existed. Most people didn't live long enough to become grandparents during the eighteenth and nineteenth centuries. And those that did probably maintained their own homes—separate from, although nearby, their grown children.

In the past, however, older people may have played a more central role in the family lives of their children and grandchildren than they do today. To account for this, experts have offered a variety of explanations which we will examine more closely in the next section. But it is incorrect to say that old people have completely lost touch with their families or, worse yet, that their families have abandoned them. Surveys show that 80 percent of the elderly see their children or grandchildren once a week. And telephone conversations presumably occur even more frequently.

The elderly and their children also rely on each other for advice in handling various problems. This can create friction, however. Some adults who like to do things their own way admit that accepting advice from parents, as they did when they were children, can be pretty hard to do. On their part, elderly parents also have trouble regarding their children as mature adults and agreeing to listen to them.

In addition to advice, the elderly report giving gifts, and sometimes money, to their children. Elderly people in lower income brackets, however, are far more likely to receive financial aid than give it. A survey in New York City also revealed that 87 percent of the elderly received assistance from their children in doing everyday household chores and in dealing with crises.

With the high divorce rate and the large number of single-parent families, more and more elderly people have assumed a major responsibility for raising their grandchildren. While this phenomenon is relatively recent among white middle-class families, it has long been common among blacks. With a single mother working and serving as the sole support for her family, a grandmother steps in to run the household. Thus, she has a clearly defined and vitally important function.

GRANDPARENTS AND GRANDCHILDREN

For most older people, the birth of a grandchild is a source of tremendous pride and excitement. As one grandparent put it, "Now I'm immortal." Today, grandparents live on, not only through one generation (their children), but a second, and perhaps a third. (About half of all Americans who are sixty-five and older have great-grandchildren.)

The relationship between grandparents and grandchildren can be a very special one indeed. It often escapes the natural tensions surrounding parent-child relationships because grandparents don't bear the primary responsibility of child rearing. They can indulge a child, even spoil it, without worrying so much about the long-range consequences. Children, in turn, seem to know that they are free to just be themselves when they're in the company of their grandparents.

As the great French philosopher Jean-Paul Sartre said of his grandfather:

> *I was his wonder because he wanted to finish life as a wonder-struck old man. What could he have required of me? My mere presence filled him to overflowing. He would call me his "tiny little one" in a voice quivering with tenderness. His cold eyes would dim with tears. He worshipped me.*

Grandparents have an opportunity to play a variety of roles in the lives of their grandchildren. Some are natural teachers who can unravel the mysteries of baking a perfect apple pie, or hooking a rainbow trout along a wooded stream. Looking back on my own grandmother, I realize that she served as an effective role model for me. Gram, as I called her, was a professional businesswoman (quite unusual for women of her generation) who ran a clothing store in partnership with my father. She worked six days a week, and they were long days, too. But Gram thrived on it, and the work apparently agreed with her because she continued to look much younger than her years. We were fast friends, Gram and I, throughout my entire childhood for, even with her busy schedule, she always set aside plenty of time for me. Today she stands as an example of what old age could be, at least for one person—active involvement in the business of life.

In addition to being role models, grandparents can also help parents and children over some of the rough spots in their relationships. Let's say a little boy feels badly because he has just been scolded by his father for misbehaving. Sometimes it helps to know that Dad did the same things when he was a child and had to be scolded for them, too.

A grandfather and his grandson enjoy a book together.

A grandparent can provide this type of perspective—offering an extra measure of understanding without undermining the parent's position as a necessary authority figure in the child's life.

Thus, grandparents can play vitally significant roles for a child—as teacher, role model, historian with a unique perspective on the family's past, and as a continuing source of love and compassion. Some grandparents function in all of these capacities, maintaining an intimate involvement in the lives of their children and grandchildren.

Others, however, choose to keep their distance for a variety of reasons. Many of today's grandparents raised their children to be independent. When they became adults with children of their own, their parents (today's grandparents) continued to follow this approach, leaving their children alone to carry out the responsibilities of parenting as they see fit. Grandparents are often afraid to become too involved, fearful that they'll be accused of meddling. Others are just too preoccupied with their own lives, restricting visits with grandchildren to holidays or special family get-togethers. Still others move away from their children and grandchildren to retirement communities, returning home only on rare occasions.

The relationship between a grandparent and grandchild also depends heavily on the attitudes of the child's parents. If problems develop between a mother and her mother, or between a father and his father-in-law, this often prevents grandparents from getting closer to their grandchildren and carrying out their traditional roles. If a couple divorces, one parent (usually the mother) often takes custody of the children; and she may prevent the father's parents from ever seeing their grandchild again. Thus, the grandparent-grandchild relationship can be entirely broken, a situation occurring far more often with America's high divorce rate. Although grandparents have gone to court in order to gain the right to see their grandchildren, they have so far met with little or no success.

DEATH IN THE FAMILY

In general, husbands die before their wives. Women have a longer life expectancy, seventy-eight years as compared to seventy for men, and they are usually younger than their husbands. About 40 percent of elderly women between the ages of sixty-five and seventy-four have been widowed; this figure rises to 70 percent for women over seventy-five.

The death of a spouse often causes severe changes in the surviving partner. The circumstances can be especially tragic when that couple has lived together for fifty years or longer. Even when death follows a long illness, the remaining spouse may still be caught unprepared. For a woman, her husband's death often engulfs her in a long and terrible nightmare. She may stumble through the funeral arrangements in a daze, her feelings numb. The mind puts up this kind of defense mechanism, called denial, to avoid coping with a reality just too horrible to bear. But this lasts only a brief time. Afterward, most widows experience a profound grief and a crushing sense of loss that often threatens to overwhelm them. A widow may rage at her dead husband for abandoning her to deal with the world alone, then feel intense guilt for having these angry feelings. Some women express a desire to follow their spouses to the grave, and periodically stories appear of wives who die suddenly only a few days after their husbands.

The majority, however, succeed in working through their grief and find reasons to go on living. Marie, whom you met in the preceding chapter, explained that following the death of her husband, her two daughters immediately decided to move back home. While appreciating their kindness and concern, Marie also realized that this type of living arrangement couldn't continue indefinitely.

"I finally called them together and told them it was time for me to make plans for my future," Marie explained. "Although they didn't agree with me, they did respect my decision."

After her daughters had departed, Marie suddenly found herself faced with the stark reality of being entirely alone for the very first time in her life. The loneliness overpowered her; and she wept uncontrollably.

Over time, Marie gradually started pulling her life together. She developed new interests on her own and changed the direction of her life. But the process wasn't easy. Special days, such as wedding anniversaries and holidays, proved extremely difficult. Marie recalled that a trip to a restaurant—a favorite place for her and her husband—brought back so many poignant memories that she had to leave before finishing her dinner. But Marie went back again and again, and each time it became a little easier, although some of the pain would never go away.

It was in this manner that I finally conquered the anxiety I felt every time I went anywhere alone where the two of us had previously gone. For some reason, though, I find it still bothers me to see an elderly couple walking together and holding hands.

Some widows and widowers find that it helps them to deal with the death of their spouse if they can share the experience with someone else. Throughout the country, programs have been developed in which elderly people can talk about their feelings with others just like themselves. In some cases, they meet with peer counselors—other widows and widowers who have volunteered to be trained for this work. During the training, these volunteers learn to be empathetic listeners, providing compassion and understanding, but not advice; for most widows and widowers have usually received more than enough advice already and don't want to hear any more.

While preparing this book, I attended a widow's support group consisting of a single professional, who ran the group, and about eight widows. Some had lost their husbands recently, while for others the period of widowhood was much longer. Nevertheless, their grief continued. As one woman explained: "It comes in waves." Another woman suffered through a long illness with her husband and finally put him in a nursing home when he took a turn for the worse. Now she blamed herself because he didn't get any better and finally died. A third widow, who had been in the group for some time, explained that she felt better now, ". . . more in touch with people again." A fourth widow recalled that her husband had always taken care of money matters and when he died she had no idea how to pay her bills or keep the checkbook balanced. But she learned, and she learned how to drive a car, too. This woman admitted that she tries to stay as busy as possible all day to keep her from thinking about the loss of her husband. When night comes, she is too tired to feel alone and falls asleep almost immediately.

One of the widows may have spoken for the rest when she said that the group gave her someplace where she could come and talk with others in the same situation. Nevertheless, it had not taken away the sorrow, which was still etched on every face, nor the sense of profound loss, which still sounded in every voice. Each of the women mourned deeply.

Among the elderly, family relationships can be rich and varied. Many of the elderly interact with their adult children sharing love, exchanging ideas, and providing each other with emotional and financial support whenever it's needed. Old people can also play important roles in the lives of their grandchildren, serving as positive role models, functioning as effective teachers, and providing unique perspectives that enrich the relationships between parents and children. Finally, the vast majority of the elderly seem to enjoy happy marriages. These are characterized by effective communication, mutual consideration, and a satisfying sexual relationship—all developed over many years of married life.

This only makes the loss of a spouse that much more difficult for the one who remains. And that person is usually a woman. Marie expressed it movingly in one of her poems:

When I think of you
my mind is filled
with happy memories,
of the way you smiled
and how your eyes glowed
when they looked at me.
How we laughed and cried at times,
while sharing joys
and sorrows,
and how we always
loved life so
and all it had to offer.
When I think of you
I can recall our last
good-bye.
I still hear you say to me
"I'll see you in a
little while."
But now that you are gone
I must begin a whole new life,
and knowing how
you loved me then,
will give me strength
to start again!

CHAPTER SIX

THE AGING
BODY
AND MIND

While writing this book, I became acquainted with a doctor named Len, a vigorous, athletic man who had reached his mid-fifties but looked much younger. In one of our conversations, we talked about aging. Len said that he considered himself to be almost the same person that he was thirty years earlier. But, of course, his mind and body had grown older, and he could detect the signs of aging. His eyes were not as sharp as they used to be. He no longer possessed the same physical strength. And when he saw an acquaintance again after a modest interval of time, it now took him a few seconds to remember that person's name.

Len's experience is typical of many people as they grow older. In their mind's eye, they remain the same as they were in high school or college. But their bodies age.

Aging is a process that continues throughout our lives. For most of us, it occurs naturally and gradually, so gradually that we may not even be aware of it. Little by little, our hair color turns to gray and may eventually become white. Wrinkles crease our brow, and tiny crow's feet frame our eyes.

The senses have also begun to decline. By the time people reach old age, they can no longer see objects as clearly, whether they are at a distance or close up. Much of this defective vision can be corrected by glasses. Other problems are not so easy to correct, however. Older people need more light to see, which makes driving at night very difficult for them. Many of the elderly also suffer from glare. This occurs when the lens of the eye becomes cloudy and yellowish, scattering light as it reaches the retina. A cataract develops if the lens becomes even cloudier and opaque, closing out sight. But cataracts can be treated through a surgical procedure which involves removing the opaque lens and replacing it with an artificial one. As people grow older, they may develop another common eye disease called glaucoma, caused by the fluid in the eyeball exerting increased pressure on the retina. Glaucoma can often be successfully controlled with drugs, but if left untreated, the disease eventually results in blindness.

As people age, hearing generally declines, too. This may be due to factors such as a degeneration of the nerve fibers, vascular changes, or damage to the inner ear. The higher frequency range is most affected, so the elderly often have trouble distinguishing words like *this, face,* or *life.* Background sounds become more disturbing for the elderly and make hearing speech more difficult than before. When talking to the elderly, try to speak clearly, pronounce words carefully, and avoid background noise. You might also speak a little louder, but not too loud, because most elderly people find this annoying and condescending. Some of the hearing problems experienced by the elderly can be improved through the use of hearing aids, or electronic implants placed inside the ear.

Other senses are also affected by old age. The elderly experience a reduced appetite because their sense of taste

*Maintaining a regimen of physical activity
is important for the elderly.*

declines. The sense of touch decreases, too, as well as the response to pain.

Almost one-half of the aged population suffers from another well-known ailment, arthritis. This is a disease of the joints, the junctions where bones come together. Generally, a fibrous pad of tissue, called cartilage, covers the ends of bones so they can come together smoothly at the joints. But as aging occurs, the cartilage wears away, and when pressure is placed on the joints—during walking, for example—severe pain may result. This is known as osteoarthritis, the most common form of the disease among the elderly. Doctors can treat arthritis with a program that combines rest and exercise, and drugs, the most widely used being aspirin. However, some of the painful symptoms will generally remain.

Osteoporosis is a bone-thinning condition that afflicts about 25 percent of women over sixty. Their bodies do not create enough new bone cells to replace the old bone cells which are lost. Osteoporosis may be caused by declining hormone levels in these women, inadequate amounts of calcium and vitamin D throughout their lives, or insufficient exercise.

As a result of osteoporosis, elderly women's bones can fracture or break more easily. Women may also shrink in size as the bones in their spine (known as vertebrae) compress, and fracture. Some women even develop a stooped condition resulting from curvature of the spine. To prevent osteoporosis, doctors recommend that younger women maintain a diet high in calcium and vitamin D, and follow an exercise program that includes jogging, walking, bicycle riding, or any other activity that places moderate stress on the spine.

As the body ages, important organs and systems begin to operate less effectively. At age seventy-five, breathing capacity has been reduced by more than one-half, and the kidneys are operating at only 70 percent efficiency. Muscle strength, which reaches its height between the ages of twenty and thirty, has declined too. The heart also operates at only about 70 percent of capacity. Meanwhile, the amount of cholesterol in the bloodstream may have risen dangerously over the years, as the result of improper diet, narrowing the blood vessels. Consequently, a sufficient amount of blood may not reach the heart to properly sustain it, or the heart may have a more difficult time pumping blood through the narrowed vessels to other organs. Eventually, the aging heart may break down, causing severe illness or even death. Cholesterol deposits can also clog the vessels carrying blood to the brain. When one of these vessels becomes completely blocked, a stroke may occur, resulting in the loss of a bodily function—speech, for example—controlled by the brain.

For years, doctors believed that all the elements of physical decline were a natural part of the aging process. But new evidence suggests that this decline, while it may be inevitable, can at least be slowed. A low-cholesterol diet, for example, can greatly reduce the risk of heart disease. According to Everett L. Smith, director of the Biogerontology Laboratory at the University of Wisconsin, 50 percent of the reduction in the heart's efficiency and in breathing capacity results from disuse, not old age. This decline can be slowed through a program of exercise carried on throughout the course of our lifetime.

Maintaining a proper weight is also important to the aging process. Obesity (extreme overweight) is a factor in high blood pressure, heart and lung problems, as well as other ailments. In addition, individuals should avoid alcohol abuse and cigarette smoking. Smoking is linked to cancer and heart and lung disease. Finally, the routine use of medical services can also help lengthen life. During regular physical examinations, a doctor can detect disease in its early stages and have a much better chance of curing it before it becomes too late.

*This man is researching his
genealogy in the library.*

In short, all of us may be able to influence, at least to some extent, the status of our health in old age by the actions we take today and in the years ahead.

AGING AND THE MIND

Do our personalities change as a result of aging? The experts disagree. Some point out that the elderly seem more cautious than young people. Others contend that today's elderly grew up during the Great Depression, an experience that instilled in them a profound sense of caution, not just in old age, but throughout their entire lives. The aged are also portrayed as being rigid, dogmatic, and unwilling to try anything new. But this may not result from aging. Some individuals carry these personality traits with them throughout an entire lifetime; they simply grow more pronounced with age. As we saw in earlier chapters, some old people eagerly involve themselves in new activities or embark on new careers. They hardly seem rigid and dogmatic. Many of the elderly, however, appear less interested in important achievements once they have retired and left the workplace. As one older person put it: "A great tension is gone . . . the fact that you don't have to compete all the time."

As people advance into their seventies and eighties, they often measure time differently. No longer do they count the years since their birth, as they did when they were younger, but count instead the number of years they have left. One woman in her late eighties even went so far as to refer to it as "the waiting," the waiting, of course, for death.

Instead of focusing so much on the future, old people may spend increasing amounts of time thinking about the past. Psychologists point out that one of the important tasks of old age is for each individual to come to terms with his or her past. Unless they can accept themselves—

what they've done as well as what they've failed to do—individuals cannot find a sense of contentment in old age. Instead, it can become a time of anger and bitterness.

Gerontologists cite other factors that seem to lead to contentment in old age. These include good physical health, financial security, and a fulfilling relationship with someone else, usually a spouse. Old age also seems to be satisfying for those elderly people who are happy with what they are doing. For some this may mean the chance to just relax and not work. But for many others, it means keeping active and involved with life. Gerontologists believe that many of the elderly are prevented from pursuing an active life-style because they suffer from low self-esteem. They feel that old people like themselves are useless to the rest of society and, therefore, they choose to isolate themselves from it. Health problems, such as poor hearing and failing eyesight or forgetfulness may also cause elderly people to be fearful about leaving home and engaging in activities with others. To help these individuals, many communities provide a variety of services which we will examine more closely in the next section.

Do our intellectual abilities decline as we grow old? Here, again, there is no clear answer. Intelligence is a complex phenomenon with many dimensions, and aging may affect each of them differently. Tests suggest that the elderly learn at a slower speed than young people do. They also seem to have greater difficulty understanding and absorbing new information, especially when it's complex, and integrating it with what they already know. This may account for some of the apparent memory problems that afflict old people. Since they have more difficulty understanding new information, they have a harder time storing it in their memories. However, once the information has been stored, the elderly have little trouble recalling it. By contrast, complex information that they learned many years earlier, during adolescence or middle age, can be recalled far more easily. In fact, old people do extremely well in that area of intelligence which is based on prior learning or experience. This so-called "crystallized intelligence" involves the use of acumulated wisdom to make judgments and solve problems.

It has also been shown that elderly people can maintain much of their mental faculties if they use them. Tests have shown that old people who remain mentally active can even increase certain types of intelligence. In short, there is no reason to believe that individuals who have led productive lives cannot also enjoy a productive old age.

The overwhelming majority of old people are not senile. Of the small minority who do suffer from senile dementia, some develop the illness as a result of a tumor or succession of strokes. In about half the cases, however, the cause is Alzheimer's disease. Alzheimer's is a degenerative brain disease which afflicts about 1.5 million Americans. Approximately 5 percent of people over sixty-five suffer from the disease. In its initial stages. Alzheimer's is characterized by small memory lapses. As the disease progresses, memory loss increases. Eventually, the individual with Alzheimer's has difficulty seeing, speaking, and walking. In time, the disease attacks all the bodily functions and eventually produces death.

Today, extensive efforts are underway to understand the causes of Alzheimer's disease and find a cure for it. But, so far, scientists have found no definitive answers.

A much more common problem among the elderly is depression. This is frequently caused by all the stressful changes occurring in their lives. Change is difficult for all of us, but especially for elderly people who have less physical strength to cope with it. The elderly must often deal with the deaths of their friends, the death of their spouses, as well as a natural decline in certain physical and mental abilities. All of these loses can prove frightening and overwhelming. They take an enormous psychological toll which may have severe physical effects, undermining an elderly person's health even further.

The result may be that the individual can no longer live independently and will require continuous medical care.

HEALTH CARE
FOR THE ELDERLY

For the elderly who are chronically ill, effective medical care often spells the difference between life and death. The family frequently acts as primary care-givers for an elderly person.

But caring for a loved one who has fallen victim to Alzheimer's disease, cancer, or a stroke can prove an extremely heavy burden. One frail, elderly woman recalled that the round-the-clock responsibility of nursing her sick husband had virtually cut her off from the rest of society. She wasn't complaining, only stating the situation matter-of-factly. And this woman had only now begun to take those first hesitant steps to re-enter society following her husband's recent death.

A survey of family members who care for elderly relatives revealed that the most difficult task was lifting an aged person; the most upsetting was helping that person with his or her toilet needs. Care-giving proved to be especially difficult for those women—and women usually fulfill this role—who also had a husband and children depending on them. In some cases, the elderly person being cared for was not even the woman's parent, but her father-in-law or mother-in-law.

A man and woman deliver a cooked meal as part of the Meals on Wheels program. This program provides the elderly and elderly invalids with regular, nutritious meals.

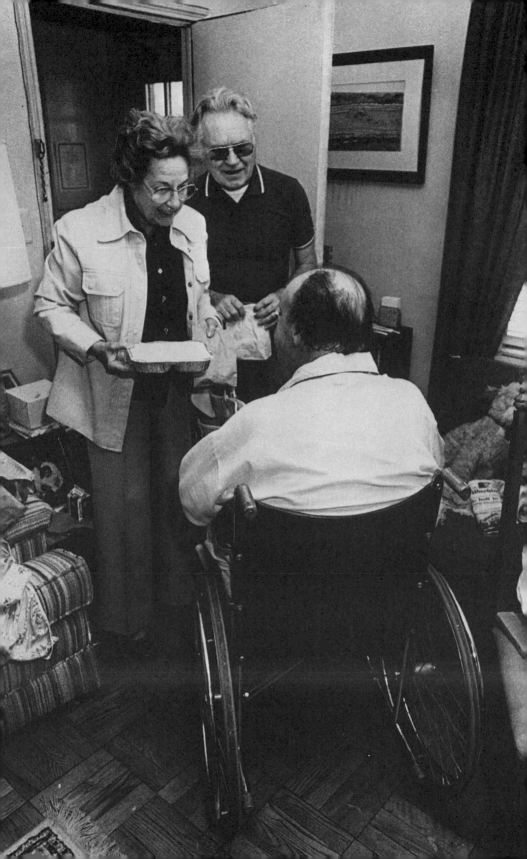

Some experts contend that the typical family assumes less responsibility for the welfare of its elderly members today than in the past. A primary reason, these experts say, is increased mobility. Jobs often force adult children to move far away from their aged parents; or the elderly, themselves, move to retirement communities in warmer climates. And even those children who continue living near their elderly parents, the critics allege, often neglect them.

Recent studies, however, reveal a different story on all counts. Not only do the overwhelming majority of the elderly live near at least one of their children, but these children are usually willing to help care for them when the need arises. As for those children who do not live close by, long distance does not necessarily imply an absence of caring. Many people try to arrange care for parents who are suffering from a chronic illness, although they live thousands of miles away. Often this task involves numerous trips and frequent visits with care-givers before a reliable program can be established. To assist with these problems, so-called "case-management" services have recently been established in some areas. These private agencies work with people in long-distance situations to help them arrange whatever services their elderly parents may need.

In recent years numerous communities have been making an effort to organize every resource available to enable elderly people to remain at home as long as possible where they can continue enjoying an independent life-style. Virginia, for example, has established the Nursing Home Preadmission Screening Program designed to evaluate elderly patients and help them avoid unnecessary stays in nursing homes. The program determines which services the patients would need to remain at home and whether these are offered within the community. In Connecticut, the Independent Living Program fulfills a similar function. Teams of medical personnel and social workers evaluate an individual's health and decide which in-home services are necessary. These could include meal preparation, help with household chores, physical and speech therapy, a live-in companion, or skilled nursing care. Next the team determines what resources exist to pay for these services, including Medicaid, social security, and the Older Americans Act. Finally, the team does a follow-up to ensure that the elderly patients are receiving all the services they need.

In some communities, adult day-care facilities have been established for the elderly who are chronically ill. Patients are transported from their homes to the facility each day, where they receive health care, meals, and psychological counseling. Centers also provide comprehensive recreation programs and offer the elderly ample opportunities to interact with others.

Over the past few years, the state of Oklahoma has trained thousands of paraprofessionals who assist the elderly with their household chores, prepare meals for them if they are following special diets, and carry out other important tasks. Some of these paraprofessionals are old people themselves. Although they receive a small stipend for their work, their primary motivation seems to be the urgent desire to help others.

In Long Beach, California, SCAN (Senior Care Action Networks) is another community program that coordinates services for the elderly. Among its members are young people from nearby schools studying in the field of gerontology. These students visit the elderly in their homes and read to them, write letters, cook meals, mow lawns, and help with other chores.

Most of the elderly want to continue living at home where they are surrounded by the familiar, in a place that truly belongs to them. These programs represent only a sampling of the efforts underway to help the elderly remain at home, independent, and part of the community for as long as possible. Far more, however, still need to be done.

DEATH AND THE ELDERLY

Although medical science seems capable of postponing death almost indefinitely, eventually the inevitable must occur. In America, the leading causes of death among the elderly are heart disease, cancer, and strokes. While most people died at home in the past, today the elderly generally live out their final hours in hospitals. Here they are surrounded by the latest in medical technology, with every effort made to keep them alive. Our society is committed to prolonging life, but the rising cost of this commitment has moved some to ask how much longer it can continue. Others wonder whether we should be concerned only with life itself, or with the quality of that life. For example, if a very elderly man with terminal cancer suddenly undergoes kidney failure, should he be placed on a kidney dialysis unit to keep him alive? Or should he simply be allowed to die? To deal with these questions, some elderly patients have made out living wills. These direct that if the patient falls into a coma and death seems inevitable, no extraordinary measures should be taken to prolong life.

An increasing number of patients have also chosen an alternative to hospital care—the hospice concept. Most of the people who come to a hospice are terminally ill cancer patients. The hospice keeps these patients as comfortable as possible during their final illness but makes no unusual efforts to prolong their lives.

Janis Casey is the administrator of the Hospice of Stamford. Connecticut. Ms. Casey explained that each patient in the hospice program is assigned a team of people who care for his or her needs at home. A nurse carries out an assessment of the patient's physical health and looks at the home environment. Usually, a terminally ill patient will have a family member who acts as the primary caregiver, Mrs. Casey said. But the hospice also provides the services of a home health aid to help bathe the patient or prepare meals, which can give family members much-needed rest. A social workers helps dying patients and their families resolve any problems that may exist between them and cope with their feelings regarding death. Physical therapists help the patient manage pain; and pastoral care is provided for spiritual needs. Hospice of Stamford has contracted with a local hospital where, if it becomes necessary, patients can spend their final hours. Some hospices maintain their own inpatient care facility.

Describing her own experiences with Hospice of Stamford, Janis Casey said:

I've had a lot of opportunity to think about my own death being here. I'd like to be home in my own bed. I'd like it to be a sunny day. I'd like to have my animals on my bed next to me. That's where I'd like to be—with people who love me and care about me.

What thoughts run through the mind of an elderly patient who has been diagnosed as terminally ill? Generally, the first reaction is shock and disbelief, the feeling that "this can't be happening to me." Patients may feel angry and bitter about their fate, while also experiencing overwhelming fears—fear of the unknown, fear of the pain that their illness will bring, fear of leaving a loved one alone. But as the disease progresses and exhausts the patient, these fears often alternate with an overpowering desire to have the entire ordeal over. Meanwhile the patient drifts back and forth between the fantasy that somehow a miraculous cure will be found for the disease, and the reality that no cure is likely.

At the same time, the elderly patient's family may be trying to resolve their own conflicting attitudes regarding the situation. For example, a son might feel sorry for himself at losing his elderly mother, then experience guilt as a result. A woman who has cared for her husband throughout his illness may feel sorrow mixed with a sense of relief that the end to his suffering is finally at hand.

As death approaches, patients react differently. Some rage against death and refuse to give into it. Some resign themselves to it, and appear to draw strength from their ability to accept the inevitable. Others derive solace from an abiding belief in God and everlasting life. And still others seem satisfied that they will no longer be a burden to their families.

There is truth in the notion, after all, that individuals face death in much the same way that they have lived their lives. Life is a complex pattern, and at each step along the way we must be prepared for change. Individuals vary greatly in their ability to cope with change—whether unexpected illness, aging, or even death itself. But our attitude toward events like these and our ability to adjust to them will greatly determine the sense of fulfillment we find throughout our lives.

CHAPTER SEVEN

THE AGED AND AMERICA'S FUTURE

In 1981, at the age of sixty-nine, Ronald Reagan became the oldest man ever to take the oath of office as president of the United States. Four years later, Reagan won reelection with the largest electoral vote landslide in the history of the republic. It was quite a vote of confidence for an "old man." And it served as still further proof that the aged can still make important contributions to our society.

In all likelihood, President Reagan will not be the last elderly American to achieve the nation's highest office. Today, more people are living into old age than ever before; many remain in relatively good physical health and most retain their mental faculties. Surveys tell us that the majority of old people enjoy comfortable or at least adequate, financial circumstances. Generally, an elderly person lives near some of his or her children and grandchildren, so there are frequent interactions between the generations. If the elderly grow too sick to care for themselves any longer, their families usually pitch in and help. Under most

circumstances, a nursing home is chosen only as a last resort.

Thus the statistics dispel some long-standing myths about the elderly: most are not poor, or senile, nor are they abandoned by their children to live out their final days in a nursing home.

However, these facts should not lull us into a false sense of complacency. For the statistics tell another story too.

Approximately 15 percent of the elderly languish below the poverty line and at least as many more totter precariously just above it. Poverty strikes some groups much harder than others. Over 17 percent of elderly white women live in poverty; this number jumps to 32 percent for black men, and soars to over 42 percent for black women. Many of the poor also lack adequate medical treatment, especially those in rural areas who must travel long distances to the nearest hospitals. Moreover, the poor often fail to receive Medicaid because some states set arbitrary standards that disqualify many thousands in the direst need.

Medical treatment—even when it is available for the elderly—may be the wrong kind, at the wrong place, and at the wrong time. Today, millions of chronically ill elderly would prefer to continue living at home and remain part of their communities. But in-home services are frequently inadequate, and since Medicaid refuses to pick up the tab for many of these services, the elderly often cannot afford them. Surveys have shown repeatedly that many of the people presently confined in nursing homes could have remained at home if only they had received adequate assistance. And this will likely continue as a major problem in the years ahead.

*President Reagan on his
visit to China, 1984*

While America has made huge strides in prolonging life, we have yet to create an environment where the elderly can enjoy the quality of life that they surely deserve.

Surveys provide an overview of the elderly population. But individuals speak far more eloquently than dry statistics. Some of the elderly who were interviewed for this book obviously suffered from heartbreak and loneliness. I spoke to women who deeply mourned the loss of their husbands and whose eyes welled with tears when they talked about the past. And I encountered a man who had found nothing to do after retirement and seemed to have lost his way.

But I met others whose lives filled me with much greater optimism. Perhaps they do not represent the majority of old people but they do exemplify what old age can be. These people were busy starting new careers, hosting their own radio programs, pursuing hobbies, and volunteering their time to enrich the lives of others. I call them the Ageless Ones. While their step may no longer be as nimble, or their eyesight quite as sharp, and while they may suffer from numerous aches and pains, they still keep on going.

What will old age be for each of us when we finally reach it? No one, of course, can predict or control the future. Chance always plays its inevitable role. Nevertheless, we can affect the type of old age we have by thinking about it, and by preparing for it throughout our lives.

Good health, for as long as possible, is essential for a satisfying old age. And we can take steps to preserve our health by following a proper diet, by exercising regularly, and by avoiding cigarette smoking, and alcohol and drug abuse.

Varied interests are essential too. If we cultivate these interests throughout a lifetime, they can enrich our old age. Attitudes are also important. An openness to life and to new experiences, can prevent the rigidity that characterizes too many people, young and old alike.

But most important are the attitudes we have toward old people and old age itself. For unless we can see ourselves in the old people around us, we will never accept the fact that we'll be old someday, too. And unless we can accept old age as just a natural part of life, we will refuse to prepare or even think about it.

Medical science has opened up new vistas, and many of us can confidently anticipate living into our eighties and perhaps longer. For us, old age need not represent the end of everything, but the opening of a dynamic new stage, albeit the final one, of life. However, this will only happen if we recognize that old people have significant roles to play in our society. As grandparents, workers, volunteers, social activists, and even political leaders, they are presently making important contributions. But there are still many others who feel left out and forgotten because America seems to believe (and the elderly often believe it, too) that there is no meaningful contribution for them to make.

Only when these attitudes change will the position of old people in our society really improve. Only then will we have created a supportive environment for today's old people and for ourselves when we reach old age. And only then will most of us begin to realize the full potential of old age.

BIBLIOGRAPHY

Beauvoir, Simone de. *The Coming of Age*. New York: Putnam, 1972.

Blythe, Ronald. *The View in Winter: Reflections of Old Age*. New York: Harcourt Brace Jovanovich, 1969.

Botwinick, Jack. *We Are Aging*. New York: Springer, 1981.

Brecher, Edward. *Love, Sex, and Aging: A Consumer's Union Report*. Boston: Little, Brown, 1984.

* Cassidy, Robert. *Margaret Mead: A Voice for the Century*. New York: Universe Books, 1982.

* Clark, Ronald. *Benjamin Franklin*. New York: Random House, 1983.

* Cowley, Malcolm. *The View from 80*. New York: Viking Press, 1980.

Crystal, Stephen. *America's Old Age Crisis: Public Policy and the Two Worlds of Aging*. New York: Basic Books, 1982.

* Fischer, David. *Growing Old in America*. New York: Oxford University Press, 1977.

Hess, Beth and Markson, Elizabeth. *Aging and Old Age.* New York: Macmillan, 1980.

Lammers, William. *Public Policy and the Aging.* Washington, D.C.: Congressional Quarterly Press, 1983.

Manley, Anne. *The Hospice Alternative.* New York: Basic Books, 1983.

Silverstone, Barbara and Hyman, Helen. *You and Your Aging Parent.* New York: Pantheon Books, 1976.

* Skinner, B.F. and Vaughan, M.E. *Enjoy Old Age: A Program of Self-Management.* New York: Norton, 1983.

Webster, Bryce and Perry, Robert. *The Complete Social Security Handbook.* New York: Dodd, Mead, 1983.

Magazines: *Aging, Modern Maturity, U.S. News and World Report, World Health, Discover, Industry Week, Nation's Business, Newsweek, Time.*

* Appropriate for high school students

INDEX

"I AM WHO I AM"

"I AM WHO I AM"

Speaking Out About Multiracial Identity

by Kathlyn Gay

FRANKLIN WATTS
New York / Chicago / London / Toronto / Sydney

Library of Congress Cataloging-in-Publication Data

Gay, Kathlyn.
"I am who I am" : speaking out about multiracial identity / by Kathlyn
Gay.
p.   cm.
Includes bibliographical references and index.
ISBN 0-531-11214-4
1. United States—Race relations. 2. Pluralism (Social sciences)—
United States. 3. Pluralism (Social sciences) 4. Racism—United
States. 5. Racism. 6. Multiculturalism—United States. 7. Multi-
culturalism I. Title.
E184.A1G34   1995
305.8'00973—dc20   94-39206
                                                           CIP AC

CONTENTS

TO RAMONA DOUGLASS,
WHOSE ARTICULATE VOICE HELPED MAKE
THIS BOOK POSSIBLE AND WHOSE FRIENDSHIP
I DEEPLY APPRECIATE

My gratitude also to Nissa Beth Gay for her help with interviews, and the individuals who have spoken out on biracial, multiracial, and monoracial identity. I am hopeful that their words will inspire thoughtful consideration of our commonalities as well as appreciation for our differences as members of one human race.

Kathlyn Gay

"I AM WHO I AM"

CHAPTER ONE

THE MANY FACES
OF PREJUDICE

As a multi-racial, multi-cultural, multi-national people we have risen from a variety of . . . circumstances. . . . We have moved in and out of history as a force recognized, as in Hawaii; denied, as in the mainland U.S.; a people who have become the norm, as in Mexico; and a people who have been relegated into absurd margins, as in South Africa and the Middle East.

> —*from the introduction to* Voices of Identity, Rage and Deliverance: An Anthology of Writings by People of Mixed Descent

On August 6, 1994, an arsonist set fire to the Randolph County High School in Wedowee, Alabama, an incident apparently sparked by a race-related conflict that began months earlier. The previous February, Hulond Humphries, the principal of the integrated high school of 680 students, called an assembly of juniors and seniors. He asked if anyone planned to bring a date of another race to the spring prom. If so, he said he would cancel the traditional event. Humphries' rationale was that schoolyard fights had erupted because of interracial dating, so the ban was supposedly a means of ensuring student safety. However, numerous black residents of the East Alabama hamlet charged that Humphries, during his twenty-five years as principal, had consistently discriminated against black students, disciplining them more harshly than whites, for example, and requiring segregated busing for students going to classes at a vocational school. Indeed, a 1989 U.S. Department of Education review criticized Humphries for various discriminatory practices. After Humphries announced the prom ban, he asked if anyone had questions. ReVonda Bowen, the junior class president and chairperson of the prom committee, asked who she was supposed to bring to the prom since she is biracial—her mother is black and her father is white. Without hesitation, Humphries reportedly told the popular sixteen-year-old, "That's just it. Your mom and dad made a mistake, having you as a mixed child." Humphries declared his ruling would help prevent interracial dating and similar "mistakes" by others.[1]

Understandably, ReVonda Bowen was distressed and began to cry, and, as she reported, "everybody else started hollering and crying." Later, ReVonda's parents, who were shocked that the principal would make such a remark, reassured their daughter that she was not a mistake, and that they loved her very much.

Although Humphries recanted his assertion the next day and announced that the April prom would take place, the Bowens and others in the community launched protests, calling for the suspension of Humphries. In mid-March, the superintendent suspended Humphries with pay pending an investigation, but the school board reinstated him at the end of the month, causing more than 100 students to boycott classes. Even before the conflict escalated, the Southern Poverty Law Center of Montgomery, Alabama, filed a lawsuit on behalf of ReVonda Bowen, claiming that Humphries' "comments and illegal policy of discouraging interracial relationships among students created a hostile environment for Ms. Bowen, violated her civil right to be free from discrimination and caused her to endure extreme embarrassment and humiliation." Morris Dees, chief counsel for the Law Center who filed the suit, said, "No school official should be allowed to infect young minds with this kind of bigotry."[2]

The school insurance company awarded ReVonda $25,000, but that did not close the case, which could be litigated further. After persistent urgings from several civil rights organizations, including the multiracial group called the Association of MultiEthnic Americans (AMEA), the U.S. Department of Justice also brought legal action in mid-May. The Justice Department charged that the Randolph County School District had not complied with two previous court orders to correct civil rights violations and asked that Humphries be removed or reassigned to another position. But that did not happen until after a fire gutted the high school on the August weekend. The following Monday, the Randolph County Board of Education removed Humphries from his position as principal and placed him in an administrative job overseeing the rebuilding of the high school.

DISCRIMINATION AND HOSTILITY

The Alabama case is only one of many incidents of discrimination against interracial couples and multiracial people. Of the dozens of interviewees for this book, all reported some instances of discriminatory acts against

[13]

them or hostility because of their mixed ancestry. Most expressed "hurt"—bruised feelings—because of name-calling or other insults or nonacceptance by peers. One student said she was "always getting into fights" at school because classmates called her names or taunted her for being of mixed ancestry. A sixteen-year-old of black-white ancestry said that in school black kids have hassled him and have told him to "stick with your own kind."

Another teenager said she was tired of people always "wanting to know if it was 'weird' living with parents of different races."[3]

Dealing with probing, personal questions is a common experience among people of mixed-race ancestry. Usually when a person's appearance does not seem to fit a particular racial category, she or he may be subjected to curious, disapproving, or even hostile interrogation. "It's like practically every day at school, someone comes up to me and asks me 'Are you Mexican, Indian, Puerto Rican?' Or they ask 'Where do you come from? Were you born in the United States?' Or 'What are you, anyway? I mean, what race do you belong to? What do you call yourself?' They can't figure out who I am because of my skin color and hair—somebody always wants to feel my hair," explained Veronica, a teenager in Lansing, Michigan.

Veronica's mixed ancestry—her mother is considered white/Hungarian; her father, who died when she was four, was African/French (considered black)—has prompted more than questions about where she belongs in terms of race. She has also been subjected to teasing and taunts. "Because I hang around mostly with white kids, some blacks call me a wannabe—I guess they don't understand I *am* part white—it has nothing to do with wanting to be. I'm also called 'zebra' a lot—and other names, too—because of being mixed." On the other hand, Veronica's sister, Victoria, who is two years younger, has encountered a different kind of inquiry.

Because of her darker skin color, Victoria said, "I

[14]

don't usually get asked what I am. People just assume that I'm black. To them I look black. They don't even think about biracial. Like, some of my friends thought I was black until they saw my sister and they said 'That's not your sister. You aren't really sisters, are you?' When I said 'yes' they ask, 'Were you adopted?' I say no, but they say 'Nuhuh, you can't be Veronica's real sister. She looks white and you're black.' I say, 'No, I'm mixed.'"[4]

A northern California teenager, Alice Wong, who is of Malaysian and American (white) ancestry calls herself "mixed" because, as she explained, "I am Asian and white, not just Asian or white." She said that because of her ancestry, she was once called "an illegitimate child during a class discussion on interracial dating." Apparently the name-caller stereotyped people of mixed ancestry as being illegitimate. Another hurtful experience, she said, occurred when she was part of a tour group traveling to Nevada. "I was made to sleep on the floor because I was Asian—I was actually told this!"[5]

Alethia Alvarado of Ventura, California, an olive-skinned teenager whose father is of Mexican descent and mother is of Polish, French, Irish, and Native American descent, said she is aware that people around her look upon people of mixed ancestry as "different" and want to categorize them some way. She pointed out that she is "pretty close" with the Mexican side of her family, but that relatives always tease her. "They like to call me names like 'white bread' because most of my friends are white."[6]

In the Midwest, Michelle Suen, a preteenager whose father is Chinese (born in China) and mother is of German and Italian ancestry (born in the United States), has often been questioned about her heritage. The questions are prompted because, as she put it, "I have my daddy's eyes." Michelle is quick to tell anyone that she is half-Chinese and half-American, but she doesn't like "kids teasing me by doing the eye thing," she said, demonstrating how classmates mock her by pulling at the corners of their eyes to reshape them.[7]

A CHANGING FACE

Until recent years, people seldom acknowledged a racially blended heritage for fear of discrimination or harassment. Certainly racist behavior and prejudice still adversely affect many people of mixed ancestry. But racially mixed people are the fastest-growing segment of the population in the United States, and their increasing number has reached a "critical mass," as some sociologists have described the phenomenon. In other words, there are enough people of mixed ancestry to be heard and read, and perhaps to make a difference in how they are perceived by the rest of U.S. society.

Beginning in the late 1960s, the number of recorded interracial marriages and unions began to rise. As a result, the number of biracial children increased, too. In 1972, for example, 2 percent of all births were children of interracial parents. But in 1991 such children accounted for 3.4 percent of all births, according to the Population Reference Bureau.

An estimated 600,000 to perhaps a total of 5 to 10 million biracial or multiracial children and adults live in the United States, although the total number is probably closer to the 5 million mark. No one knows the exact number of multiracial Americans, because no nationwide count has been taken. In the 1990 U.S. Census, some people wrote in their ancestry or checked a box labeled "Other," which usually indicated that the individual was of a multiple or biracial ancestry. But no category yet exists on U.S. Census or other federal government forms for multiracial people.

Counted by the Census or not, Maria Root, a clinical psychologist in Seattle, Washington, whose heritage is both racially and ethnically mixed (she is of Filipino,

Spanish, German, Portuguese, Chinese, and Irish ancestry), is convinced that "The emergence of a racially mixed population is transforming the 'face' of the United States."[8] This is confirmed in studies conducted by researchers, who themselves are of mixed ancestry and represent diverse disciplines. Some of their findings are part of the 1992 publication *Racially Mixed People in America*, which Root edited.

Other evidence of a changing face appears in several nationally distributed magazines: *Interrace*, initiated in 1989; *New People: The Journal for the Human Race*, first published in 1990; *Interracial Classified*, launched in 1992; and *Biracial Child*, introduced in the winter of 1993–94. All four publications consist of feature articles and news for and about interracial families and people of mixed racial heritage. And they frequently focus on issues related to racial identity— biracial, multiracial, or monoracial—as well as race-related stereotypes.

RACIAL IDENTITY AND STEREOTYPES

When people select a racial category for themselves, they identify their genetic heritage and perhaps use one of the current classifications: Black, White, Asian, Pacific Islander, American Indian, or Alaskan native. Or some people might place themselves in the Hispanic category, indicating they are part of a group that shares an ethnic background and a cultural heritage, such as the same language, religion, and customs. But a person of Hispanic heritage might also be classified as any one of the designated races.

The topic of racial categories can create heated debate, because there is no universal agreement on what "race" really means or how humankind should be classified. In the first place, every classification system has been devised by a person with a particular point of view based on a specific discipline—usually

[17]

anthropology or biology. Classification systems also are political inventions. In an essay titled "The Illogic of American Racial Categories," historian Paul R. Spickard of Brigham Young University in Hawaii, pointed out that "race, while it has some relationship to biology, is not mainly a biological matter. Race is primarily a sociopolitical construct. The sorting of people into this race or that in the modern era has generally been done by powerful groups for the purposes of maintaining and extending their own power."9

Although racial classifications systems have varied considerably over the years, there is agreement that all people belong to one species, *Homo sapiens*, with genetic material that is similar. But over thousands of years, populations have adapted to certain environments, and visible differences among people have developed that have been passed down in the genetic structures. Those outward physical characteristics have been used to classify separate populations into groups known as races.

However, there may be more variations within a categorized group than between different racial groups. Skin color is a prime example. Some people who are classified as "white" may have skin color that is darker than people classified as "black," and a person who is categorized as "black" could have a skin color ranging from pale pink to ebony. At the same time, one racial group may share genetic characteristics with another group—blood type, for example. In fact, "genetic differences between the so-called races are minute," writes Paul Hoffman, editor in chief of *Discover* in an editorial, "The Science of Race," for a special November 1994 issue on the topic. Hoffman notes that "race accounts for only a minuscule .012 percent difference" in the genetic material of all humans.

Gordon W. Allport pointed out years ago in his classic work *The Nature of Prejudice* that "(1) Except in remote parts of the earth very few human beings belong to a pure stock; most [humans] are mongrels (racially speaking). . . (2) Most human characteristics ascribed to race are undoubtedly due to cultural diversity and should, therefore, be regarded as ethnic, not racial."[10] Members of a group learn behaviors from their families and the larger culture within which they live, rather than inherit them.

STEREOTYPES AND RACISM

Frequently people confuse learned traits with inherited characteristics. Sometimes learned characteristics are applied to all members of a group, creating stereotypes. When negative stereotypes are applied to racial groups, they support racism. By one definition, racism is the use of power by a dominant group to discriminate against a racial group categorized as "inferior."

Prejudicial views have also affected the kinds of studies conducted on and conclusions reached about racial groups and people of multiracial ancestry. For example, in the past researchers generally accepted both popular and academic beliefs that individuals of mixed-race heritage were destined to be "problem" subjects, so their studies were designed with such ideas in mind and often came to predetermined conclusions.

By contrast, dozens of recent studies by multiracial people and members of interracial families who represent diverse disciplines have focused not only on people with problems but also on those who function well in society. Such investigations conclude that many negative assumptions about mixed-race people are simply wrong. Most important, people of mixed ancestry—just by being themselves—have counteracted myths about racial mixing, and many individuals have shown that they are healthy, positive, constructive people who want to be acknowledged—and appreciated—for their multiple or biracial mixture.

[19]

CHAPTER TWO

ROOTS OF RACIAL CONCEPTS

Greetings! I am pleased to see that we are differ-
ent. May we together become greater than the sum
of both of us.

> — A Vulcan greeting from the
> TV series "Star Trek"

Over the centuries, people have developed a variety of
methods for categorizing themselves. For example, in
many parts of the world, genealogy (family lineage) has
long determined a person's status in society.

The ancient Greeks divided people into separate
groups. Only landowners could be citizens; conquered
people from other lands or Greeks who could not pay
their debts became slaves. In feudal societies in Europe
people were separated by class, with serfs at the bottom, merchants in the middle, and the nobility at the
top. In India there has long been a very strict caste system, with Brahmins at the top and untouchables at the

bottom. Various economic class systems are still found in most nations of the world, including the United States.

Although people may be divided into higher and lower classes within a society, they may also be united by a common way of life. People who are part of a particular culture may believe their way of life is superior to any other. Such a belief, called ethnocentrism, has caused people throughout history to label any "outsiders" as "barbaric" or "uncivilized" or "less than human," even if those in the "out-group" happen to be the same race. For example, ethnocentrism is a major factor in wars between African peoples, between indigenous groups (those native to the land) in the Americas, and between ethnic groups in parts of Europe, such as Northern Ireland and the former Yugoslavia. Perhaps the most horrendous expression of modern ethnocentrism was German Nazism.

RACIAL LABELS IN THE AMERICAS

Ethnocentrism and the acquisition of power and dominance were factors responsible for the use of racial and color labels to categorize and enslave people in the early Americas. Spanish and Portuguese colonizers of what is now known as Latin America first enslaved indigenous people, and then imported Africans as slaves. The British and Dutch helped spread the practice in the West Indies and North America.

To justify slavery, Caucasians (light-skinned Europeans) looked upon people of color as "inferior," considering them "heathens" and attributing every manner of negative quality to those they considered "subhuman." Classifying nonwhite groups as "inferior" helped maintain, as well as justify, the economic and social dominance of the white group in power in the early Americas as it does in U.S. society today. As historian Paul Spickard explained: "Putting simple, neat racial labels on dominated people—and creating negative myths about the moral qualities of those peoples—makes it easier for the dominators to ignore the individual humanity of their victims."[1]

Religion also played a role in reinforcing negative images of those in nonwhite racial categories. Some Christians preached that slavery could be justified on the grounds that the enslaved were being "saved" from their "paganism" and were "happy" in their subservient roles. Many white religious leaders declared that dark-skinned people, particularly Africans, were cursed by God, carrying that curse through the ages, an erroneous assumption.

BIOLOGICAL THEORIES

During the 1700s European biologists began to classify all living things according to a pyramid system, from kingdom at the top to genus and species at the base. Ethnocentric and racist ideas led some researchers to decide that the species *Homo sapiens* (humans) should include subdivisions of distinct racial types. A *Typological Theory*, as it was called, determined race by the geographical location and the physical appearance of people, such as skin color, the type and color of hair, the shape of the nose and lips and the shape and color of the eyes.

According to one British sociologist, the *Typological Theory* supported a widely held belief that "the growing economic and political strength of the European powers sprang from qualities inherent in the white race, or races" [white Europeans of different nations were often considered separate races]. Those qualities supposedly "promised continuing European supremacy."[2]

The false notion of inherent European superiority provided a basis for ranking racial categories by gradations of color, placing the lighter-skinned people, such as Europeans at the top. Next in the ranking system were Asians and then Native Americans, with Africans at the bottom. Such a system supported the myth that whites inherited "superior" intelligence and "superior" moral sense, and nonwhite groups supposedly were born "innately inferior." Various intelligence tests and studies were conducted in attempts to "prove" such notions.

During the 1800s, for example, an Italian doctor, Cesare Lombroso, spent years making minute measurements of human skulls to determine whether members of a racial group had the same skull shape and size and whether these biological characteristics were linked to a specific group with criminal tendencies. His ideas were accepted by many Europeans and Americans, who wanted a reason—no matter how mistaken it might be—to label another group as "inferior."

Scientists today denounce the idea of measuring skulls in order to link biological factors to criminal behavior, since research has shown that criminal behavior often stems from social factors. But some researchers are still trying to blame events such as riots and other social upheavals on biology.

In 1992, Fred Goodwin, a psychiatrist and then director of the U.S. Alcohol, Drug Abuse and Mental Health Administration, announced federally sponsored research in this area—a program called the "violence initiative," which would attempt to find genetic factors marking children as violence-prone. The racist approach to the research became apparent when Goodwin described the violent behavior of young male rhesus monkeys, then immediately compared this behavior to black males in the inner city. In his words, "Maybe it isn't just the careless use of the word when people call certain areas of certain cities jungles."[3]

[23]

Because of his remarks, Goodwin was fired from his job, but he was appointed director of the National Institute for Mental Health (NIMH). In October 1992, the NIMH planned to hold a conference at the University of Maryland titled "Genetic Factors in Crime: Findings, Uses and Implications," which is part of the violence initiative. But psychiatrists from the Center for the Study of Psychiatry, a nonprofit organization dedicated to reform in the psychiatric profession, organized an information campaign that helped stop the conference. According to psychiatrist Peter Breggin, who heads the Bethesda, Maryland, center, the biomedical approach to the study of violence

> *distracts the nation from the true sources of pain, suffering and violence within the inner city. . . . [It] is the most recent example of a remarkably consistent viewpoint that has recycled in modern history at critical periods of social conflict in the United States and Europe. It rationalizes social ills in biomedical terms that blame the victim—in this instance the young inner city Black man—by declaring him genetically and biologically unfit. Claims for a biological and genetic basis for any form of human conduct. . . have been made for several hundred years despite an utter lack of evidence. The claims survive . . . because they are fundamentally political rather than scientific.[4]*

BANS AGAINST RACIAL MIXING

Racism and ethnocentric beliefs also were a basis for some of the early bans against miscegenation—usually defined as "interbreeding" between groups (races) of people presumed to be distinctly different. The early Europeans who explored and conquered the Americas at first had cohabited with Native American women. This was for practical reasons because few European women were part of the early expeditions to the Americas. On some occasions, though, there was mutual attraction. As men and women have done since the beginning of human history, couples fell in love, married, and produced children.

When slavery was introduced, many slave women were forced to comply with white men's sexual demands. Seldom was a female slave able to get beyond her early teenage years without being raped or seduced by a white "master" or his sons. The mixed offspring that resulted usually became slaves.

Free people of color and whites also intermixed, adding to the number of mixed progeny. In the Louisiana territory the children of unions between French or Spanish colonists and Africans became known as Creoles of Color or simply Creoles (although many in Louisiana of European ancestry would argue vehemently that the term *Creole* refers only to those of mixed French and Spanish descent). When Asian men came to the United States to work as laborers, many intermixed with people of European, Native American, and African ancestry.

As people of mixed racial ancestry matured and bore children, multiracial people multiplied hundreds of times over. Many North American colonists became alarmed that their so-called white racial purity was being "contaminated." Even though many colonists were of hybrid stock themselves—from many diverse backgrounds—they passed laws against miscegenation.

The Maryland colony passed the first antimiscegenation law in 1691. Then through the time of the American Revolution and the Civil War, most U.S. states enacted legislation banning interracial marriages and unions. Once again, there was no rational argument for banning interracial marriages, and people acted on the basis of their racist beliefs.

Antimiscegenation laws were in force in thirty states just after World War II and upheld in sixteen states until the 1960s. Not until 1967 did the U.S. Supreme Court declare the last state antimiscegenation law in Virginia unconstitutional.

State laws in the past seldom barred a person of color (labeled as black, brown, yellow, or red) from mixing with someone else of color. However, before the Civil War, some slaveholding states prohibited unions between Native Americans and free or enslaved Africans. State officials feared that if people of African and Native American descent merged, Indian nations would support slave uprisings. That fear also prompted some states in the Southeast to encourage and help establish slaveholding among several Indian nations.

Still, many Native Americans supported slave uprisings or provided refuge for runaway slaves who then were adopted by the Native American group. In fact, research shows that from one-fourth to one-third of African Americans have Native American ancestors.[5]

The European and American taboo against interracial unions appears ludicrous in the face of historical accounts clearly showing that groups of people have migrated across continents and intermixed for thousands of years. During ancient times, middle European nations were conquered and the natives intermixed with Asians and Mediterranean peoples, including Romans, Spaniards, and Huns. Germanic tribes intermixed with those they conquered or with the varied groups who conquered them. Arabs and Moors (who were a mixed group of Africans, Berbers, and Arabs) occupied Portugal and Spain for several centuries, inter-

[26]

mixing with these populations. Italians have intermixed with Africans and people of Arabic-speaking nations as well as with the French, Swiss, and other Europeans. Before exploration of the Americas, the Portuguese, Spanish, Italians, Dutch, and other Europeans conquered and colonized along African coastal areas, intermixing and producing racially mixed offspring.

Mixed-race people throughout history have contributed to science, technology, culture, and many other aspects of life that benefit all of us. Hundreds of people of mixed ancestry fought in all of America's wars, including the war for independence and the Civil War. One Revolutionary War hero was Crispus Attucks of African American and Native American heritage. Orator and freedom fighter Frederick Douglass was of mixed African, Native American, and European ancestry. Poet Langston Hughes's ancestors were African American and Native American.

HOW TABOOS ARE REINFORCED

In spite of such a heritage, racist views prevailed in the early days of the Americas, and antimiscegenation laws were enforced in the United States. But the legal sanctions and taboos against interracial mixing did not stop the practice. So government officials and the clergy frequently urged citizens to look to biblical passages for guidance. The meanings of many of these passages were twisted to support arguments against interracial marriages. For example, the biblical phrase "What communion [or fellowship] has light with darkness?" was quoted to "prove" that light and *dark* people should not mix.

Although the entire passage (2 Corinthians 6:14-16) clearly deals with the contrast of good and evil, it has been misinterpreted and applied to people on the basis of their skin color. This is true in part because of the negative perceptions of "darkness" that have persisted for thousands of years, providing a basis for light-skinned people to apply negative labels to dark-skinned people.

The negative connotations associated with the colors black and brown and the term *dark* have become part of the English language, and, in fact, black is defined in dictionaries as an adjective symbolizing a range of calamitous or dishonorable if not downright "evil" events. Such terms as "black list," "black sheep," "black day," "blackmail," and "blackball" are just a few of the dozens of expressions that by association have linked negative attributes with people of dark skin color.

On the other hand, the dominant white society developed numerous positive connotations for white, associating the word with fairness, honesty, and reliability. According to sociologist Irving Lewis Allen, "In the nineteenth century, a white-Indian was a "good Indian" . . . a white-man was a native, not an alien; a gentile, not a Jew."[6]

Clearly, people impose their own values on a color, and the symbolism associated with a color varies from one culture to another. In some parts of Asia, for example, white symbolizes death and is the color of clothing worn to funerals. Dark colors may symbolize the bounty of the Earth in other cultures. A color is neither good nor bad, positive nor negative; it is simply a word that describes things. Color certainly has nothing to do with the quality of a person.

CLASSIFICATIONS FOR MIXED-RACE PEOPLE

White supremacist ideas spawned more than racial/color categories that ranked and stigmatized people. They also were the basis for the many classifications for offspring of interracial unions.

Centuries ago, Europeans developed an elaborate system for differentiating people according to their degree of African or Native American ancestry. That system was adopted in Latin America, where most of the population today is of mixed heritage. However, various classifications for racial mixtures do not necessarily carry a stigma.

In the past, North Americans adapted the Latin American system to create rigid distinctions between whites and nonwhites. The color coding was part of the institution of slavery and was designed to ensure that children born of a black/white union would be slaves. Such categories also were used to bar free people of color from voting or owning property.

During the 1800s, anyone of half-white and half-black heritage was commonly labeled mulatto (from the Spanish *mulato*, the word for hybrid and also donkey or mule, a half-breed animal); quadroon for one-fourth black; octoroon for one-eighth black. Another "intermediate race" consisting of people with black and Native American heritage was labeled sambo (from the Spanish *zambo*). The sambo term also was used to classify people of mulatto and black heritage. Anyone of one-sixteenth black heritage was labeled griffe, and the classifications continued, identifying even one sixty-fourth black heritage.

The U.S. Census Bureau used such classifications until after the 1890 population count. At that time, Booker T. Washington, of black/white ancestry, convinced the Census Bureau that all people of African heritage should be classified as Negro, a term which is offensive to many people today because it is linked to the demeaning, insulting term *nigger*. Although the Census Bureau dropped the mathematical distinctions for people of black/white heritage, general use of these terms continued well into the twentieth century and the term *mulatto* is still commonly applied today.

[29]

The absurdity of the classification system is apparent when one considers the fact that it is impossible to measure whether a person inherits one-half, one-fourth, or any precise fraction of a particular genetic makeup. Even if it were possible to determine an exact percentage of "blackness," "whiteness," or whatever, anyone of black/white heritage who was considered to be one-sixteenth black, for example, would logically be fifteen-sixteenth white. So, if the system were logical, that person would be white.

But the classifications were not designed to be logical. They were a way for whites to label anyone with a fraction of black heritage as black, commonly known as the "one drop of black blood" rule. In white-supremacist jargon, that meant the person with a drop of black blood was "inferior" and of low status.

No similar one-drop rule applied to Native Americans, Asians, or others categorized as nonwhite. There were variations of that rule, however. For example, people of Indian and white ancestry were sometimes disparagingly called "half-breeds." And anyone who "looked" Indian or could be linked to Indian ancestry would automatically be considered nonwhite and perhaps labeled a "free person of color" or a "mulatto," no matter what his or her heritage.

Through the years, groups other than whites also have adopted the one-drop rule. For example, some groups of African ancestry have insisted that anyone with any "black blood" should label himself or herself black. People of African ancestry as well as those of Native American heritage have used terms such as "blood" or "blood line" or "blood relative" to indicate either an inherited connection or a shared culture or both.

However, a combination of many factors determines the blood type a person will have. Genes, not blood, are the biological units that transmit hereditary traits. Scientists have only recently begun to map and code the estimated 100,000 genes that each human cell contains.

COUNTERACTING FALSE THEORIES

Since about the early 1900s in the United States, various researchers have assumed that all or the vast majority of multiracial people are unstable — "mixed up and messed up" in today's jargon. As a result, the researchers usually have found evidence to support their false assumptions. But some recent studies have shown that while psychological or social problems may be blamed on a mixed-race ancestry, in many instances those problems stem from such factors as poor self-esteem, family stresses, and the underlying racism in U.S. society that can affect almost anyone labeled non-white.

A related myth says that biracial or multiracial people are supposedly destined to lead unhappy if not miserable and tormented lives and will meet tragic ends. Myths, after all, are fiction, so they have been used to develop characters in literary works by authors ranging from Shakespeare to William Faulkner to modern novelists. Yet a few recent stories as depicted in film, and described in more detail in Chapter 6, have debunked the myths, showing biracial people in strong, positive roles.

Another conjecture from the past that has survived to this day declares that people of mixed ancestry are "marginal," living on the edge of society, never accepted in any particular group. As a result, according to the false notion, offspring of interracial unions supposedly are doomed to a lifelong quest to answer the question "Who am I?" But that is a question that many people, no matter what their heritage, try to resolve. And people of biracial or multiracial ancestry develop a positive concept of identity as often and perhaps earlier in life than many other individuals in society.

The myths about people of mixed ancestry are difficult to eliminate. This is true in part because Americans generally don't get to know racially mixed families or people and their strengths. Unfortunately, the misconceptions also are part of a system that still allows privileges to those who are "white."

Some people of mixed ancestry struggle to keep from internalizing the misconceptions that society dumps on them, but others challenge the stereotypes and myths. Increasingly multiracial people are speaking out about who they are and informing the public at large about how they cope in a racist society.

CHAPTER THREE

COPING WITH
RACISM

It is not easy to be part Red, part White and part
Black; part oppressed and part oppressor; part
have and part have-not. I feel . . . the primitive
struggle between love and hate, us and them,
same and different, acceptance and rejection,
pluralism and racism.

> —*Linda J. Mahdesian,*
> *"I Am America,"* Melange
> *(September 1989), p. 3*

When Allison Joseph, a Vassar College student, was still
in high school, she wanted to find out how people of
racially mixed ancestry similar to her own coped with
prejudicial attitudes and behaviors. Joseph explained:
"My father is white, descended from Russian Jews who
lived in an area invaded long ago by Asian peoples.
Judging by the shape of my father's eyes, his ancestors

[33]

may have had interactions with the Mongols or others of Asian heritage. His mother is German-Jewish. My mother is black and her family is also mixed: there are Native Americans, Arawak Indians, African Americans and western Europeans in her background."

Joseph reported that her mixed ancestry has prompted only a few prejudicial incidents, which in her opinion, might be due to the fact that she appears "white." As an honors project at Bronx High School of Science in New York, Joseph developed and conducted a study entitled "The Effects of Racism on White-Appearing Children of Integrated Marriages." For her study, described in a 1992 issue of *Interrace* magazine, she interviewed ten young people of mixed ancestry, aged fifteen to twenty, who reported a variety of reactions from classmates and others.

Several girls said that boys found them attractive because of their "exotic" or "interesting" looks. Most respondents said their mixed backgrounds evoked "surprise and sometimes suspicion" from their peers. One teenager felt that her biraciality created tension between herself and others of a single racial background; she thought that people went out of their way not to offend her with racist remarks. Nearly all of the respondents in Joseph's study had experienced some form of discrimination or prejudicial comments. Three respondents said they "consistently experienced discrimination when in public with their darker-skinned parent." But all had learned to cope, which in Joseph's words, "is necessary to avoid getting hurt by racist behaviors."[1]

HELPING YOUNG PEOPLE COPE

Learning to cope is not always a simple matter, however, since some people encounter racist acts that include name-calling, teasing, taunts, and threats of violence against them. Ideally, young people of mixed ancestry have parents who help them combat abuse from those who disapprove of their blended heritage. Such parents are advocates for their children, finding ways to help their offspring gain self-esteem and to be proud of their racially mixed heritage. The parents also work with schools and teachers to combat prejudice about their children's mixed ancestry.

In a study of forty-four young adults of black/white heritage in California, clinical psychologist Agneta Mitchell found that those who identified themselves as biracial had a strong sense of who they were. They felt "they belonged in both worlds" rather than just to one racial group or to no group at all. Mitchell reported that many of the biracial adults had experienced anxiety due to "a lot of stuff from teachers and kids"—put-downs, teasing, and harassment. But, according to Mitchell, once the biracial young people in her study "got through the stress" they became "really healthy" individuals.[2]

If some multiracial individuals, like people of any other group, are unable to get "through the stress" of daily living, they may seek help in counseling. Levonne Gaddy, a psychotherapist, works with such young people. Gaddy helped found Multiracial Americans of Southern California, a support network, and she also helped develop the Center for Interracial Counseling and Psychotherapy in Los Angeles.

Gaddy, who is of African, Cherokee, and European ancestry, attended all-black schools when she was growing up in North Carolina but was constantly teased and harassed because of her light skin color, hair, and gray-green eyes. She said she always "felt different" but considered herself a black person and no one could tell her otherwise. But that identity changed when she went to an all-black college in North Carolina. As she explained:

During that time I went with a friend to a Black Muslim temple and heard the minister talk about ugly, blue-eyed devils. Even though I identified as black, I knew the minister was talking about part of me. I sank lower and lower in my seat as the minister talked on and on about the evils of white people. The minister then looked over the audience and said: 'Fear not, all you light people out there. Your whiteness was raped into you.' That was a turning point for me, because I knew that my whiteness had not come from rape and that my white ancestry came from the female side of my family. So from then on I started to examine my own racist attitudes—black against white— and began to acknowledge all of my heritage.[3]

THE "DOUBLE WHAMMY"

As pointed out by many of the young people inter-viewed, one of the problems that people of mixed ances-try may face is hostility from both the dominant and minority groups. At a 1992 meeting of multiracial stu-dents at the University of California (UC) Berkeley, a young woman whose mother is of Japanese ancestry (born in Japan) and father is of African heritage (born in the U.S. South), told the group that she is not accepted wholeheartedly by either the Japanese or African-American community. She is often made to feel "different" because "[p]eople think it's so tragic you have to be two things. . . . They just see totality as being one thing. . . . In order to be a whole person, I have to accept both [heritages]."[4]

That is a concept that Terry Wilson, professor of Native American Studies and Ethnic Studies at UC Berkeley, frequently emphasizes in his classes, particularly in his seminars on "People of Mixed Racial Descent." Wilson explained that his point of view developed because of his own Potawatomi and French-Canadian heritage. He was born on a Kansas Indian reservation but when he was four years old moved with his family to Oklahoma. There he lived within an Indian community of Arapaho and Cheyenne, where he was plagued with taunts about his ancestry.

"In the public school, both white and Indian guys would call me half-breed or just 'breed,' and I'd end up getting right into their faces and beating those faces into a pulp. I'd get into nearly maniacal fights trying to stuff those insults down their throats. My sister and parents always told me that if I ignored the taunts the boys would stop bothering me. But I thought: if I hit the guys enough then they'll stop bothering me!" Wilson said. He explained that his parents did not provide guidance in dealing with mixed-race issues because "it was something people didn't talk about." As a result, he continued fighting over taunts until one day he lost a battle with three boys and ended up in the hospital, battered. He recalled:

When my father came to visit me in the hospital he told me he was kind of glad I got beat up—not glad I was hurt, but, he said, 'You needed to learn that you can't whip everybody and you have to find different ways to deal with the problem' although he didn't say what the problem was! For me it was the beginning of a more balanced way of looking at life. I began to realize that I did have to find different ways to deal with the fact that I was a mixed-race person in a society and culture that does not want to acknowledge my existence.

[37]

Wilson's transformation came about during his under-graduate and graduate studies in history, when, he said,

I learned that people had been lying to me and the books I had been reading about being mixed race, about being a half-breed, had been lying to me. In my study of history I learned that those persons who were of Indian and white or Indian and black heritage were not unfortunate indi-viduals caught between two cultures with no place to go—as the books said—but just the oppo-site was the case. Those mixed-race individuals almost to a person were accepted into the vari-ous tribal societies and became especially val-ued members of those societies because they had a huge advantage. They were biracial, bicultural, and bilingual.

As a result, Wilson noted, those of mixed ancestry were able to communicate and deal with people from a vari-ety of cultures. This is a concept that Wilson now passes on to students and others, exhorting individuals of mixed heritage *not* to let everyone else decide who you are but instead to "toughen up and tell them who you are!"[5]

Another Californian of German and Chinese ances-try came to a similar conclusion, but not until she had gone through a great deal of psychological conflict and confusion. Caren (not her real name) and her experi-ences were described in an academic paper on people of mixed ancestry written by Michelle M. Motoyoshi, who wanted to test the validity of various theories about multiracial individuals. She conducted in-depth inter-views with three women, one of whom was Caren.

Motoyoshi explained that Caren attended a "pre-dominantly White elementary school in San Diego, [and] was one of only two people of color in her class.

. . . She was called 'Chink' and 'Chop Suey' more times than she can or cares to remember. The children, by deriding her, made her feel different, even weird. . . ."

Caren also experienced discrimination during her teenage years when she lived in San Francisco's Chinatown. According to Motoyoshi:

Whites predominated at the school [Caren] attended during the week. There she was ostracized because she was the only Asian around. At Chinese school, on the other hand, she was considered White and was teased because she did not look and could not speak Chinese. As a result . . . Caren viewed herself as an outsider . . . like a misfit.

[She began to associate] primarily with Whites and meticulously emulated their behavior. She lightened her hair. She avoided sunlight for fear of becoming dark-skinned. With the help of lemon juice, she tried to bleach her skin and give herself freckles. Her desperate attempts to be White, however, did not result in her feeling happier or whole, but rather made her even more anxious and self-conscious about her racial background.

After Caren entered college, where she became part of a supportive group of mixed ancestry, she "learned to accept herself and to take pride in who she was," Motoyoshi reported. "[Caren] learned that to be whole, she had to acknowledge she was 'half' and that there was nothing shameful about being so."[6]

Although the other two women Motoyoshi interviewed did not appear to suffer psychological conflicts, they reported being shunned by "cliquish" racial groups and feeling like outsiders at times. But Motoyoshi found that the two women (and others like

[39]

them) were able to cope with discrimination and the negative messages that society sends about intermixing in part because their families accepted and encouraged multicultural contacts and helped them develop self-esteem.[7]

Elizabeth Atkins, a journalist with the *Detroit News*, is a prime example of a person who has developed coping skills—among them confidence in her own self-worth and a sense of humor—to deal with harassment and discrimination because of her mixed ancestry. In an article for *New People* magazine, she described herself as "a multiracial black woman with long blond hair, green eyes and white-looking skin. With a black mother and white/Native American father, my social and political identities are African-American. But people who judge me on appearance without knowing what I'm all about, especially black women, are angry when they see me with black men. They cut piercing, evil eyes at me, blurt mean comments and whisper angrily to each other while staring at me and my man."

Atkins reported numerous incidents in which she and a male black friend had to deal with the "evil eye" of blacks or ugly insults from whites— "a double whammy of hostility," as she described it. In the past Atkins felt self-conscious about her light skin and upset when black people "couldn't tell that I'm black too." But, she reported, "at age 25, I've finally learned to ignore these incidents or laugh away the pain and anger." In her view the incidents were, and still are

> *spawned and fueled by vicious, rampant racism that ravages the black community both externally and internally. From white society, we face racism every day. It gnaws at and corrodes our self-esteem while feeding bitterness and anger toward whites. And among African Americans,*

a deep-rooted obsession with light skin fosters a
self-destructive, stifling and divisive mentality
that hinders our political and social agenda . . .
this won't change until blacks overcome the belief
that white standards of beauty—long hair, light
skin and light eyes—are superior to darker skin,
kinky hair and broader features. With hope, the
emerging Afrocentric pride will remedy that.[8]

"COLORISM"

Atkins's experiences are similar to those described in *The Color Complex: The Politics of Skin Color Among African Americans*, which explores "colorism," or intraracial discrimination based on skin color. The book was initiated by Kathy Russell, who is "a Black woman with fairly light skin and long hair," as she described herself. Russell wanted to investigate the kind of color bias she experienced as an adolescent. Her research led to Midge Wilson, professor of women's studies and psychology at DePaul University in Chicago, and Ronald Hall, assistant professor of social work at Augsburg College in Minneapolis, both of whom had studied the "color complex."

The threesome brought together, in their words: "the perspectives of a Black woman, a White woman, and a Black man on the enormously sensitive topic of skin color and feature discrimination among Blacks." With numerous anecdotes and statistical information, they reveal that

Traditionally, the color complex involved light-
skinned Blacks' rejection of Blacks who were
darker. Increasingly, however, the color complex
shows up in the form of dark-skinned African

[41]

Americans spurning their lighter-skinned broth-
ers and sisters for not being Black enough. The
complex even includes attitudes about hair tex-
ture, nose shape, and eye color. In short, the "color
complex" is a psychological fixation about color
and features that leads Blacks to discriminate
against each other. . . .[9]

The origins of "colorism" and color bias in the black
community can be traced to the days of slavery, when
color coding became part of the racial classification
system. During the slave era, light-skinned slaves often
were sold for high prices at auctions, and some were
even bred for that purpose. Usually light-skinned slaves
were household servants, while darker-skinned slaves
were relegated to field work and other hard labor. After
slavery was abolished, light-skinned blacks frequently
gained more privileges than people of darker skin color,
and many rose to positions of power. Through the years,
light-skinned blacks became an elite group, and the
perception developed that light-skinned blacks could
advance economically, socially, and politically far easier than those of darker hue.

According to a 1992 reader poll conducted by *Ebony*
magazine, about half of those surveyed still believed
that light-skinned blacks were favored, while the other
half thought the perception false. The magazine editors cited some evidence to support the perception that
light-skinned blacks are more favorably treated than
dark-skinned blacks. One example was the "word from
many adoption agencies . . . which report that a continuous stream of Black couples—most with mid-brown
to dark complexions—express an overwhelming pref-
erence for light-complexioned or mixed-race children."
Another indicator was a recent study showing that

"darker skinned Blacks still face a greater degree of social and economic barriers, with darker skinned Blacks earning sometimes up to 50 percent less than lighter Blacks with similar educational backgrounds and occupational status."[10]

Some people with dark skin try to escape what they view as color bondage. One forty-one-year-old schoolteacher in Philadelphia explained it this way:

> *I'm what folks down South call "blue," as in so black, I'm blue. My grandmother told me if I washed myself in milk it would lighten my skin. So that's what I did every day, and I started convincing myself that I was actually getting lighter. I had been raised to believe that skin color, even among black people, really mattered in how you did in school, what job you got, where you lived, who you married and, basically, what kind of life you would have.* [11]

In attempts to deal with some of the debilitating effects of negative attitudes about skin color, an increasing number of people are speaking out on color stereotypes. Contemporary black authors such as Alice Walker, Maya Angelou, and Itabari Njeri, and journalists, playwrights, TV script writers, and entertainers have dealt with the subject of colorism in recent years. As the authors of *The Color Complex* stated, they want to help "heal some of the wounds the color issue has inflicted on the African-American community."[12]

THE HAWAIIAN EXCEPTION

About the only part of the United States where mixed ancestry is sometimes celebrated is in the state of

Hawaii. There mixed ancestry is a well-accepted fact of life. Descendants of Polynesians (who first settled Hawaii), Japanese, Chinese, Korean, Filipino, Portuguese, Europeans, and other groups have learned to share traditions. People of mixed ancestry are now the largest population group in Hawaii.

Hal Glatzer, a journalist for the *San Francisco Chronicle* who worked in Hawaii for eleven years, noted that "After two centuries of living together in close quarters, people in Hawaii . . . know how to relax around people who are different. . . . [Hawaiians] have found it economically, politically or socially unprofitable to be racist."[13]

However, that does not mean Hawaiians have eliminated categories for people. Those who are part Asian and part Caucasian think of themselves and are considered by others to be *hapa heole* (part Caucasian). Those whose heritage may include Asian and Polynesian are known as cosmopolitan or local—not of the mainland. The local category carries with it higher status and "is vastly more important, in social relations, than one's ancestry. Being local implies that one is family centered, concerned with consensus more than accomplishment. . . . Race and ethnicity are trivial compared with the distinction between local and nonlocal," according to sociologist and psychologist Ronald C. Johnson of the University of Hawaii.[14]

Unfortunately, as is clear from the incidents already described, people of mixed-race ancestry on the U.S. mainland must still struggle with the issues of race and ethnicity. A special 1993 issue of *Time* magazine on "The New Face of America" states:

> *During the past two decades, America has produced the greatest variety of hybrid households in the history of the world. As ever increasing*

numbers of couples crash through racial, ethnic and religious barriers to invent a life together, Americans are being forced to rethink and redefine themselves.[15]

Certainly many people of mixed-race ancestry in the United States are a catalyst in that process, especially when they insist on recognition of their integrated identity and emphasize a shared culture: a diverse and constantly changing American culture.

CHAPTER FOUR

I AM
WHO I AM

I am not white, black, Asian, Hispanic, or Native American. . . . I am multiracial and I do not want to pass as "Black" or as "White" or as anything but a human being.

> —Jamoo, of Cherokee-Spanish-white-black descent, in "Passing for White: The Outing of Mixed Race People," Interrace (September/October 1991), p. 28

Children and adults of mixed ancestry may be told countless times that they will face conflicts over their identity. Such counsel frequently comes from people who believe that a person has to accept a one-race model for self-identification. Increasingly biracial or multiracial people are showing by example that they do not suffer a lifetime of confusion about who they are.

[46]

Many people of mixed ancestry emphasize that self-identity is an ongoing process—that a person's definition of self changes periodically, depending on the developmental stage of one's life. For example, Melissa Hunter of California, whose father is black and mother is white, said that "a few years ago I felt society had isolated me—that I was very different. I felt all alone and didn't know who I was. Sometimes I just didn't fit in with any group—like Mexican kids or white kids or black kids. But I've since gained a lot of friends of different backgrounds and now I know that I'm loved by a lot of people. I know I'm mulatto—that's what I call myself—and I'm proud of it! I don't know how it feels to be black or white or anything else. I only know what it's like to be mixed."[1]

The process of forming an identity begins to develop in early childhood and continually evolves well into a person's adult years. An individual acquires a meaning of self through family and interactions with relatives, friends, and others in the immediate community. A racial identity starts to develop early in childhood also and is shaped within the family. But that self-concept may be challenged by concepts about race and color that have little to do with who a person truly is. In addition, identity can be influenced by multiple factors such as one's gender, abilities, and appearance.

Lucas Young of Colorado, who is of Vietnamese and African-American heritage, has almost always thought of himself as black because he "looks" African American, not Asian, and knows very little about his Asian heritage. His first three years were spent in a Vietnamese orphanage, and at the age of three he was adopted by a white American family living in a primarily white suburban community in Colorado.

Young reported that during his high school years in the late 1980s, he often forgot about his "other race," which could sometimes make him feel guilty, but for the most part he has not suffered psychologically because of his mixed ancestry. He has been subjected to racist comments and slurs, but he has constantly reminded himself that some people do not know any better because "that's how a lot of them were brought up."[2]

CHOOSING A SINGLE-RACE CATEGORY

Some child development experts, sociologists, and others insist that in order for people of mixed heritage to be well adjusted, they must choose to relate to one culture or accept an identity determined by appearance. Many other segments of society agree, and pressure people of mixed heritage to choose exclusive membership in one race.

A district court judge in New York who is "a child of two multiracial parents" explained that he was raised during the one-drop of black blood rule and has always identified as black. In his view "it is a mistake to not select one race. You will find yourself being ostracized by people of both races and they will secretly act against you to your detriment." His advice to people of black/white lineage was to "choose or lose" and to "stop trying to be something that you are not."[3]

On the other hand, Adham Sawaad of Flushing, New York, a member of the Society of Haam, wrote: "I don't believe at all that Mixed Race People should be classified with The Blacks/Afrikan Americans. It doesn't look or feel right. . . . I feel that we should respect ourselves as who we truly are and that this would make for a better world."[4]

Some parents of African ancestry whose children are of mixed heritage believe their children should be taught to identify as black because that is the way many in society, including many in black communities, see them. Such parents also believe that identifying their children as black is part of the process of teaching their children survival skills—how to cope with those who perceive them only in a negative manner—and help them build self-esteem in spite of obstacles.

Wei Bie Chuan, of Chinese and white ancestry, is convinced that identifying with his minority heritage is crucial to self-esteem. He stated: "It was only by calling myself 'Chinese' that I learned what that meant." Part of that learning process was to "reconcile a Chinese heritage . . . to embrace a fate of humiliation, siege, and turmoil . . . a psychology of inferiority at least 300 years old." In his opinion, both parents of a mixed offspring may pass on "specific inhibitions against the minority identity. A Chinese parent may have struggled with a lifetime of 'not fitting in,' and may understandably want the child to avoid these troubles." At the same time, a white parent might feel that a child who identifies as Chinese will become distant and alienated. Thus, by not accepting the minority status, parents contribute to an offspring's inability to cope with "that part of himself which is most suppressed."

According to Wei Bie Chuan,

> *A half Chinese who grows up in America does not need to be told how to be an American. . . . What needs more encouragement is how to be Chinese. Which is to feel yin and yang; to read writings that are not just letters but ancient pictures of part of himself; to utter words that wrench him with the echoes of the planting of rice and the clashing of sabres for over 5,000 years; to glimpse the memory of hundreds of poets and philosophers; and to identify directly with elderly Chinese, whose presence embodies these echoes and memories. . . .*[5]

[49]

OTHER PRESSURES TO CHOOSE

Some demands for a single-racial identity come from those who believe biracial or multiracial people are "selling out" to the white culture if they do not identify with a minority group. Michelle Marie Breaux of New Orleans, who is of "Cajun-French, English, Cherokee Indian, and African descent," explained: "I am extremely proud of my mixed heritage and I wouldn't exchange it for the world. All of my life I've been mistaken for . . . [being] Puerto Rican, Mexican, Colombian, Peruvian, Tahitian or Polynesian, Filipino, American Indian, Arab, . . . [or] white with a real good tan. I am caramel complexioned Multiracial with wavy-straight long dark brown hair and have Caucasian features (pointy nose, thin lips). . . ."

Even though Breaux proudly identifies herself as a Multiracial American, she pointed out that many people insist "if you are part Black you should be labeled as Black and that people who choose to be Biracial/Multiracial are trying to escape their Blackness. How can you escape your Blackness if you are part Black? It is virtually impossible!"[6]

The Black-is-Beautiful and Black Power movement of the 1960s and 1970s and the African Nationalist movement of recent years have prompted many of African ancestry to revive the claim that anyone with a drop of black blood is black. This kind of labeling, some argue, helps preserve a culture and reverses the European emphasis on white "superiority." The emphasis on "blackness," proponents say, also helps reverse the practice of ignoring accomplishments of African Americans and other people of color.

G. Reginald Daniel, a professor in Latin American and Afro-American Studies at the University of California at Los Angeles, explained that this reversal sometimes appears justified because of the "'whitening out' of the African presence in history." But in his view, classifying people by a single category helps maintain the racist concepts that brought about the classification system in the first place.

Daniel, whose heritage includes a blend of African, French, Native American, Irish, Jewish, and East Indian ancestry, objects to applying the black label to everyone of part-African ancestry. As he wrote, "I have spent the larger part of my life seeking to resist society's one-dimensional image of both my ethnic background and identity, and replace them with a more accurate multidimensional one." To "blacken out" a person's "multiple and blended cultural and genetic origins" is no more truthful than whitewashing, he maintained, advocating instead a concept that uses terms such as "partly," "mostly," or "both/and" for multiracial identity.[7]

The concern that intermixing will diminish distinct cultures is shared by other groups, whether those groups are categorized by skin color, national background, or religious affiliations (such as Jews and Muslims). Some sociologists and other scholars in the past attempted to prove that intermixing among diverse groups eroded or destroyed cultures, but more recent studies have shown otherwise.

Amy Iwasaki Mass, a sociologist and clinical social worker at Whittier College (California) who works with Asian American families, reported "a marked increase in the rate of intermarriages" among Asian Americans, which has been "especially notable in the Japanese American community." As a result, many Japanese Americans fear the trend will destroy the Japanese community in the United States and "that Japanese Americans will become completely assimilated into mainstream America and lose their sense of community and ethnic identity." However, Mass noted that studies conducted during the 1980s "suggest that inter-racial Japanese Americans do not lose their sense of identity; in fact, they may be more aware of their Japanese heritage because they have to struggle to affirm and come to terms with their dual racial background."[8]

Mass also conducted her own study and came to similar conclusions. She found that people who struggled with conflicts about their mixed heritage attributed some of their inner turmoil to such factors as negative messages from family members about race and ethnicity and not being accepted at times by either Asian or American groups. Those who felt positive about their dual ancestry and identified with their Japanese culture as well as the American lifestyle usually had supportive, open-minded families. Being accepted in the Japanese community as part Japanese also helped interracial Japanese Americans strengthen ethnic ties and, in Mass's view, this is a major factor in helping to sustain the community.[9]

People of mixed heritage also are pressured to be counted in one of the minority groups in order to maintain federal and state government funding for programs for minorities. Government funds, for example, support many financial aid and educational programs for disadvantaged minority students attending colleges or universities. Such programs help a great many young people who otherwise would not be able to afford to earn degrees beyond the secondary level. But the programs also perpetuate the concept that only a single racial or ethnic identity is valid. The issue is especially complex in regard to those who claim to be part American Indian, or Native American. Federal and state governments and tribal groups provide millions of dollars annually in financial aid for people of Indian ancestry. In recent years, an increasing number of students have claimed Native American heritage based on one-fourth, one-eighth, or one-sixteenth, or some other fraction of "Indian blood," but education officials have found some of those claims to be fraudulent. Thus school administrators have been trying to find ways to determine whether a student's self-identification is valid.

Asking students to prove their Native American ancestry could be discriminatory since similar proof is not required of those who self-identify as black, Hispanic, or Asian. Yet leaders of some Indian nations urge that Indian ancestry be challenged, because those who falsely claim Indian heritage take away needed services and benefits legally appropriated for tribal groups.

NATIVE AMERICAN IDENTITY

The question "Who is Indian?" is a concern that goes well beyond those administering financial aid in schools. "No more knotty issue preoccupies Indian America than that of identity," says Terry Wilson, UC Berkeley professor. He explained that "few, if any, Native Americans, regardless of upbringing in rural, reservation, or urban setting, ignore their own and other Indians' blood quantum [percentage of Indian ancestry expressed in fractions]." At the same time, many object to the concept of blood percentages because it stems from racist classification systems imposed by Europeans. In the past, people of part Indian descent did not distinguish differences in terms of blood quantum but instead identified with a tribal group.[10]

Today, if a person claiming Indian ancestry is not known as a member of a particular family, or tribal group, then that person is suspect among Native Americans until his or her lineage is precisely explained or proven. In order to verify ties with a tribal group, a

[53]

person may have to show a blood quantum card that specifies percentages of "Indian blood" determined by family or tribal records.

Those of "mixed blood" who claim an Indian identity—rather than a biracial or multiracial identity—may do so for a variety of reasons, one of which is similar to that expressed by members of other groups: to prevent cultural extinction. Since members of Indian nations long have intermixed with European and African groups, many historians and anthropologists from colonial times on have declared that Indians were becoming part of mainstream America and were disappearing as a distinct racial and cultural group. But in recent years, researchers have refuted this notion and, in Wilson's words, "have demonstrated that . . . Indian communities continue to maintain viable identities."[11]

One way that Indian communities have survived is through intermarriage with non-Indians who are accepted as tribal members. Another factor in Native American identity is legal recognition of tribal groups and Indian nations. Self-governing Indian nations operate within federal government guidelines, but they are not under state government jurisdiction. Tribal groups hold land rights established by treaties with the U.S. government. But, as is well known, federal and state government officials over the years have ignored many of these agreements, and Indian nations have filed lawsuits in recent years to restore their rights.

Indian tribal identity is also maintained through powwows and other festivals that celebrate a group's customs, including many religious ceremonies that involve music and dance. These festivals also help preserve crafts. A prime example is the annual week-long celebration of the Chumash culture in southern California shared by those of Chumash ancestry and non-Indians alike.

For about 10,000 years, the Chumash lived on islands off the Southern California seacoast, along the coast, and in mountainous regions surrounding what is now Santa Barbara, Ventura, and San Luis Obispo. Like most California Indian groups, the Chumash were forced off their lands by Spanish invaders who had established empires in Mexico and later by Mexican and American settlers. Spanish missions were set up in Chumash territory from 1772 to 1804 to convert Indians to Catholicism, playing a major role in diminishing Chumash culture. Undoubtedly these efforts also resulted in intermixing of the Chumash with those of Spanish and other European ancestry. Today an estimated 1,500 people claiming Chumash ancestry still exist, and they have revived traditional cultural activities such as basket weaving and wood and bone carving.[12]

Whatever the forces that preserve Native American identity, the concept of self-identification as Indian may not necessarily mean excluding identification with another group. Some who claim part-Indian ancestry feel comfortable and accepted in both the Indian and non-Indian cultures. They appear to possess what Wilson calls "a third positive dimension" that comes from being bicultural—they are "150 percent" people.[13] This means that other biracial or multiracial people can achieve that same added dimension, integrating all of their heritage.

"EVERY SIDE IS OUR SIDE"

The labels people use to identify themselves can be "powerful tools, feeding pride or doubt," according to anthropologist David Stevenson at Wayne State University, Detroit. He believes that "a sense of control is crucial to identity" and individuals or groups should not have to accept a "right" name or terminology or a pseudo-scientific designation for who they are.[14]

Eric Tate, a student at UC Berkeley, whose mother is Japanese (born in Japan) and father is of African-American ancestry, said he was raised on U.S. military bases in the United States and abroad where there were many young people like himself—of mixed heritage. So he felt no pressure to choose one particular group, and never felt torn or confused about his multiracial identity.

"I'm black-Japanese," he said. "I was happy with that identity. Everybody else seemed happy with it. But when I came to Berkeley, I was sometimes pressured to identify as a black person. I was forced to really think about this issue [of choosing sides]. And I realized that the rest of the world may not be as comfortable with who I am as I am comfortable with myself. I now try to develop responses to questions about my identity, so I can educate others" about what it means to be multiracial and multicultural.[15]

When choosing a multiracial identity, individuals sometimes declare that "every side is our side." Underscoring that point, a California teenager, Brian Harris, whose father, Smitty, is black and mother, Barbara, is white, often speaks out publicly—at conferences and on national TV programs—about being biracial. During one Southern California seminar on interracial and biracial issues held on a college campus, Brian presented his view that "people should be proud to claim both races." Afterward, he reported, "I was confronted by four young black men around 16 to 18 years old. They were very rude and told me I need to go with my dominating roots, etc. I remained calm because they are entitled to their own opinions. I feel strong enough about who I am that ignorance does not get to me. . . . I realize I will never be able to change society totally, but I will continue to speak to change narrow minds and try to end prejudice in my generation."[16]

Audra Johnson, from Indiana, whose father is of German heritage and mother is of Cherokee and black ancestry, strongly supports that view. "When people ask about my background I always tell them I'm mixed, even though they usually want to label me 'black.' I'm not ashamed that I am part black, but I am also not ashamed that I am part white. . . . I refuse to pick sides for anyone. . . . I am who I am, and until people decide to change their narrow-minded view of the world, I am just going to have to continue to remind them."[17]

CHAPTER FIVE

"MIXED" FAMILIES

My children are Polish, Irish, African and Native American. They're multiracial and multiethnic and that's how I identify them because that's what they are.

—Pat Edwards, Washington, D.C.

"I am [of] multiracial, multicultural and multiethnic background. My mother is Italian-Puerto Rican and black [and] my father is Irish-Italian, Chinese and black. I am 32 years of age and have two children. . . . I was fortunate in that I was raised with a conscious awareness of my background and my heritage and I try to raise my children the same way."[1]

William Yung of Staten Island, New York, expressed the attitude of many people who are part of multiracial families. They may be headed by a single parent or two parents. They may be families that have formed through remarriage (stepfamilies) or through adoption.

[58]

Whatever their makeup, multiracial families may encounter difficulties in family communication, but contrary to popular opinion, the parents are not at great risk of breaking up because of conflicts over racial differences. A Chicago counselor, who conducted a survey of married black/white couples to determine how various stress factors affected their marriages, reported in 1988 that interracial couples did not experience any greater stresses than did their counterparts—married couples who were both white or were both black. Divorces were no more likely among interracial couples than among same-race married couples.[2]

SOME OBSTACLES

Perhaps some of the most difficult problems with which multiracial families have to cope is disapproval of close relatives. Numerous surveys in recent years have shown that many U.S. parents do not object to their children dating someone of another skin color, but they draw the line when marriage is proposed. Even if parents grudgingly accept their child's interracial marriage, they may ask the tired old question: What about the children? When the question is asked, the underlying assumption usually is that the children produced will not be accepted by one racial group or the other and will suffer great psychological harm.

In some cases, close relatives—including grandparents—may disown the multiracial family, literally slamming doors in their faces and shunning them for months, years, or even a lifetime. Being cut off from extended family members can be distressing and painful. Horror stories have been told about relatives who make life miserable for multiracial families, sometimes putting so much pressure on couples that the two buckle under the criticism and split up. On the other hand, multiracial families often work hard to develop healthy relationships with relatives, and many couples have found that their parents become more accepting when grandchildren are born.

Another common difficulty that racially blended families face is public curiosity and sometimes hostility from strangers. Families frequently are subjected to stares in public places or to ugly racist remarks. If a child in a family is darker or lighter in skin tone than a parent, strangers are likely to brazenly ask a mother or father, "Is that child yours?" Some dark-skinned mothers with youngsters of mixed heritage have been mistaken for "nannies" or even accused of trying to steal someone else's child.

Some mothers of biracial children have reported that they have been frequently mistaken for adoptive parents. "It's irritating," one Washington, D.C., mother said, "because people believe that the children couldn't—or shouldn't—be my biological offspring. It's even worse when someone gushes and tells me what an upstanding citizen I am for adopting 'kids like that.' I always want to scream back: 'Kids like that are going to take over the world someday,' but I try to save my energy for more positive efforts—like raising my children to be healthy, responsible adults."[3]

Celia Cuomo of California has taken another kind of approach when strangers ask if she is the real mother of Osaze Martin Cuomo, her biracial child. She reported: "I appreciate the opportunity to speak freely about this subject with others, especially in the presence of my son. He needs to know that I openly acknowledge and discuss his racial heritage. . . . [He] is a mix of cultures. Osaze is a Nigerian name meaning 'the gods like him.' Martin is after Martin Luther King, Jr. Cuomo is my maiden name, an Italian name originating in a small village outside of Naples, Italy. . . . Osa sees interracial families as normal and common. . . . 'We are related to everyone in the world. 'Everyone is in our family.'"[4]

RACIST ATTACKS

While some strangers can be annoying or rude, others can be intimidating, sometimes accosting families on the street and verbally berating couples for being together and having children. Some multiracial families have been physically attacked by white supremacists and other racists.

In 1994, the Southern Poverty Law Center, through its Klanwatch Project, reported record increases in the number of hate groups and incidents of hate violence since the beginning of the 1990s. More than 200 skinhead and other neo-Nazi organizations have been identified and are known to be concentrated along the East coast, in Southern California, and in metropolitan areas such as Chicago and Detroit, while Klan activity is heavy in Florida and Georgia.[5]

White supremacists attack primarily people of color, with black Americans the most often victimized, according to a 1993 report from the Federal Bureau of Investigation (FBI). Religious bigotry prompted 19 percent of the hate crimes, which were committed against Jews, Muslims, and other non-Christian groups. Although no statistics were available on the number of racially mixed families that have been victims of hate violence in recent years, reports of such incidents have appeared in newspapers across the United States.

In 1991, the *San Francisco Examiner* reported the four-year ordeal of one interracial family, the Drumrights in Contra Coasta County. Douglas Drumright, a Marin County employee and part-time minister who is black, and Marcia Drumright, a pediatric nurse who is white, and their four children endured a "campaign of harassment—verbal assaults, threats and annoying, often destructive pranks" against them. The perpetrator was a neighbor, Brent Case. According to the news account, Case, who was in his thirties, was "a self-proclaimed member of the Ku Klux Klan and Aryan Brotherhood." Beginning in 1987, he was responsible for "too many incidents to detail."

The newspaper reported a few examples: Case confronted one of the Drumrights' sons and threatened to "beat your black nigger father to a pulp . . . ; cursed out another son and then scratched the letters F.U. into the son's car door; poured motor oil into the family swimming pool; [and] tailed Marcia Drumright as she drove Shaina [the youngest child] to school, eventually spitting on her car, yelling obscenities and threatening, 'I'm going to get you. I'm going to get your whole family.'"

Because of the attacks over the four-year period, the Drumrights became virtual prisoners in their own home, afraid to go outdoors except when going to work or school or on errands. Drumright feared his family would be physically harmed and that their home would be burned down, so he did not retaliate, although over the years he made at least fifteen calls to the sheriff's department. No police action was taken, however.

Apparently the authorities did not take the complaints seriously. Finally Marcia took her case to the Human Relations Commission in the county, and a staff member contacted the sheriff's department. Case was arrested, tried, and sent to prison, and the Drumrights filed a lawsuit against Case, claiming compensation for civil rights violations.[6]

In January 1993, the Drumrights settled their case for an undisclosed sum. A restraining order against Case requires that he stay at least half a mile away from the Drumrights and the school their daughter attends.

CONFLICTS OVER MULTIRACIAL ADOPTIVE FAMILIES

Racially blended families formed through adoption—many of which include biracial or multiracial children—

also may have to cope with discriminatory acts and conflicts over acceptance in society. Transracial adoption—adopting children whose racial ancestry is different from the parents—has long been controversial. Critics contend that such families should not be formed in the first place. They believe that foster children (in tax-supported programs that pay foster parents to provide temporary homes for children) and prospective adoptive children should be placed with families who are similar to them in race and culture.

The political pressure to match adoptive children and parents by race did not become a matter of widespread controversy until the 1960s. Prior to that time most adoption agencies were designed to serve primarily white families, placing white infants with childless couples of northern European heritage. But because of lower birth rates and because more single white women kept their babies rather than release them for adoption, the number of babies whose birth parents were both white steadily declined. Some white couples began adopting children from Asian and Latin American countries. That practice has continued, because many couples have encountered fewer problems and less delay in forming such a family than in trying to form an adoptive family with American-born children different in appearance from the parents.

Although adoption agencies during the 1960s finally began to concentrate on minority youngsters who needed services, the agencies began to place these children primarily with white families, making little effort to find adoptive parents among people of color. The consensus among white social workers was that black and other families of color did not meet white middle-class standards for adoptive homes. But this notion has been challenged repeatedly by organized minority groups. Some of the first challenges came about during the civil rights movement of the 1960s when

[63]

African-American and Native American groups began major efforts to match adoptive children with families who shared their heritage. Since 1972, the National Association of Black Social Workers (NABSW) has adamantly opposed placing black children with white families, claiming such placements destroy children's racial identity and amount to cultural genocide—the extermination of blacks as a group. The NABSW in recent years has been pressuring Congress to pass a National Black Heritage Child Welfare Act, which would be similar to the federal Indian Child Welfare Act (ICWA). The ICWA was designed to correct past injustices against Native American families. Often Indian children on reservations were removed from their families, primarily because white social workers believed poverty, crowded living conditions, and children under the care of extended family members (rather than parents) were symptoms of a dysfunctional family. The federal Indian Child Welfare Act (ICWA) requires that a tribal council determine with whom an Indian child will be placed for foster care or for adoption.

The NABSW and tribal councils and some Asian and Latino groups continue to press for racial matching in adoption because they fear that adoptive white parents will not instill racial or ethnic pride in children of color. Some black social service workers also claim that there are black families willing to adopt, but that agencies do not seek or encourage prospective black parents. They argue as well that white parents cannot teach black children the coping skills they will need to survive in a society that demeans blacks. Indeed, some white parents use a color-blind approach to raising children, seldom if ever mentioning that an adopted child's appearance is different from that of the rest of the family. They hesitate to talk about race because they believe they will give their children negative ideas. Or they contend that being part of a loving family is all children need to develop self-esteem. But such an approach can create conflicts because children learn early in life that people are categorized by skin color and that anyone who appears different may be singled out for taunts or other types of prejudiced behavior.

Opponents of transracial adoptions also contend that children of color will have identity problems and lack a sense of belonging if they are placed in white homes. But for the past twenty years, research has shown that transracially adopted children adjust as well or sometimes better than those adopted by look-alike families. Harvard law professor Elizabeth Bartholet reviewed numerous studies that compared transracial adoptees to adopted and biological children in same-race families. She found that "All of these comparative studies show transracial adoptees doing generally as well as the other groups of children in terms of various traditional measures of social adjustment." She noted, however, that many of the researchers concluded their studies in a "cautious and negative tone," expecting that the transracial adoptees would have problems in a later stage of development. According to Bartholet,

> The early studies focused on adolescence as the point when the anticipated problems might manifest themselves. But as successive studies have followed the children through adolescence and into early adulthood, they find that the children continue to feel good about themselves, to enjoy good relationships with their families, and to do well in the outside world. [7]

Although matching adoptees with families who appear to be racially the same may be an ideal arrangement, that policy can be a form of discrimination that is outlawed by provisions of the Civil Rights Act of 1964. Title VI of the act prohibits child welfare agencies from using race, color, or national origin as the *only* basis for placement of a child with a foster or adoptive family, a fact frequently stressed by the National Coalition to End Racism in America's Child Care System (NCERACCS). The organization has helped some families fight and overturn state laws or social service policies that bar transracial foster care and adoptions.

NCERACCS, which formed in 1984 as a state group in Taylor, Michigan, now has nationwide membership. The group has called attention to the fact that many children are being deprived of homes and prospective parents are being deprived of adopted children because of racial/ethnic matching policies. As Carol Coccia, president of NCERACCS, stated: "All things being equal, like-race adoptions are best for children, but transracial adoptions should be allowed when same-race adoptive or foster parents are not available." Coccia and her husband have been foster parents for years, and they along with many others know that children suffer when skin color is the sole factor in the choice of where they will be placed.[8]

Some children may move from foster family to foster family or may wait for years in institutions before matching adoptive parents can be found. Or the children may spend their entire childhood in the foster-care system. In order to satisfy advocates of racial matching, some children have been placed with foster or adoptive parents or relatives who have been negligent and physically abusive or addicted to alcohol or other drugs. In some tragic instances, children have been fatally injured after being placed in abusive families because social service agencies insisted on same-race adoptive or foster homes. Certainly, abuse has occurred in all types of placements as well, but the point is that racial matching does not guarantee that a child's best interests will be served.

[66]

THE EFFECTS OF COLOR MATCHING ON MULTIRACIAL CHILDREN

Children of mixed ancestry available for adoption almost always are categorized as nonwhite according to their skin color. Many adoptive children designated as black, for example, are actually biracial, usually black/white. Thus because the child is categorized as black, and not as mixed-race, adoption agencies operating under color-matching policies often try to prevent couples of white ancestry or of two different heritages from adopting children of mixed ancestry.

For example, in Hennepin County, Minnesota, an infant of black/white parentage was released for adoption and placed with a white foster family, Debra and Robert Mick. Later the birth mother, who is white, signed an affidavit clearly stating that she wanted the child to be adopted by the Micks. When the child was nearly two years old, the county social service agency, which had ignored the Micks' request for adoption as well as the biological mother's affidavit, decided to place the biracial child with black foster or adoptive parents. The agency, which is required to search for relatives who might adopt the child, made no attempt to contact the birth mother's relatives and even though, as the agency conceded, the child's foster family had provided excellent care, workers recommended that the child be placed with an unrelated individual who had had no previous contact with her.

The Micks filed a complaint with the U.S. Department of Health and Human Services Office for Civil Rights (OCR), which found a mass of evidence clearly demonstrating that the agency "engaged in racially discriminatory practices in the course of attempting to remove a biracial child from white foster parents. . . ." The OCR ordered the agency to

Refrain from taking or recommending further action with respect to the child's removal unless the agency can document that the actions it proposes are in keeping with the child's best interests; and [to] amend existing policies and procedures to assure that: transracial placements are not prohibited or discouraged; race, color, or national origin is not the primary consideration in placement decisions; and children are not restricted in terms of the racial or ethnic characteristics of families considered for placement unless there exists documentation developed on a case-by-case basis that establishes a given child's need to be placed with a family of a particular race, color, or national origin.[9]

Similar cases involving controversy over placement of multiracial children as well as children of single racial heritage who are available for adoption have been reported all across the United States. However, numerous adoptive multiracial families that are not color-matched have formed successfully. In such families, adoptive white parents stress that their children of color need to be in environments where they develop relationships with other children and adults from similar cultural backgrounds. Tara Tieso-Battis, who works with prospective adoptive parents in St. Paul, Minnesota, and her husband, both of whom are white and have adopted a multiracial son, declared:

Children of color are entitled to a full sense of who they are and where they've come from. They have the right to a warm and ongoing connection with a diversity of people, who, along with their parents, can help light their path through life. They deserve a rich environment where they can learn about themselves, and how to live in

[68]

*harmony with others. . . . I know my husband
and I couldn't do it without our friends of color,
and the interracial and intercultural families we
know. They give us a sense of rightness about
our family, and they keep us real.*[10]

TAKING A POSITIVE APPROACH

Whether racially mixed families are formed biologically
or by adoption, many parents use a variety of positive
parenting strategies. For one, families try to live in areas
where there are people of diverse cultural backgrounds
or to take part in activities of multiracial and multicultural organizations.

Within a family, parents who help their children
develop in a healthy manner attempt to provide accurate information about such social issues as prejudice,
stereotypes, and discrimination. Parents help educate
their children's teachers and others in the community
about racial issues and supply their children with books,
games, toys, dolls, workbooks and other materials that
include people of mixed heritage. Parents also encourage their children to talk candidly about race and to
express their feelings about how rude remarks from
insensitive individuals sometimes affect them.

Along with talking openly about racial issues, many
multiracial families try to help their children develop
integrated identities. Francis Wardle, a family psychologist and director of the Center for the Study of Biracial
Children in Denver, Colorado, frequently writes and
speaks on multiracial family issues and advises on positive parenting skills. Wardle, who is of British ancestry and his wife Ruth Benjamin-Wardle, who is of
African, Native American, and Asian descent, have fos-
tered in their four children a deep appreciation for their
multiple ancestries.

[69]

The Wardles believe, as do many other parents of biracial children, that they "have a right and moral duty to challenge society's narrow definition of the racial identity of their children. . . ." In Wardle's view, "an inclusive definition of identity . . . [helps] children develop a stronger, more cosmopolitan, and richer sense of self-worth. The pride interracial children have in both parents' heritages and the pride the parents have in their children helps to create a strong, secure identity."[11]

When children are allowed from an early age to embrace all of their multiracial heritage "they do just fine . . . the children display a high sense of self-esteem," said Nancy Brown of Los Angeles, president of Multiracial Americans of Southern California (MASC), a support group. Brown, who described herself as "German/Jewish by heritage and a first-generation American," and her husband, who is African American, are helping their two children to appreciate their diverse ancestry. The Browns, along with other multicultural families, often are accused of denying a portion of their children's heritage, but as Brown stated, "That is not true . . . families bend over backward to try to educate their children on the different parts of their culture."[12]

In Maryland, Janice Lorenz, a black mother of two children whose father is white, told a news reporter a few years ago that her children sometimes had problems explaining their mixed heritage to friends, but she repeatedly pointed out to her children that they were interracial. She told them, "For some people that may be a problem, but you are who you are." She stressed that it is a mother's natural instinct to protect. But "The bottom line is we can't always protect, so we have to equip."[13]

CHAPTER SIX

STEREOTYPES IN THE MEDIA

. . . America has . . . distorted our story much the same way as it has distorted other non-European-American-based images on the "Silver Screen," in the "Press," and on the [TV] tube at home. . . . What we've been bombarded with is not only symptomatic of our nation's inability to face itself in "black and white," but is also indicative of our reluctance to affirm the beauty, integrity, and substance of any culture reflected outside of the pseudo-American vanilla consciousness depicted daily in the mass media. How can we expect to find our own faces in the American portrait when everyone else's is, at best, merely a pencil sketch of reality?

—Ramona Douglass, president of the national multiracial organization Association of MultiEthnic Americans (AMEA)

[71]

As multiracial families and individuals attempt to define themselves in a positive manner they must contend with dramatic film and television stories and novels that have long portrayed interracial couples and people of mixed heritage as inherently maladjusted, miserable, and doomed. Numerous newspaper and magazine articles and TV and radio talk shows also have given the impression that people of mixed ancestry have psychological or social adjustment problems, ignoring the vast majority of biracial people who have considered themselves well adjusted.

STRUGGLES TO COUNTERACT THE MYTHS

Maia Benjamin-Wardle, a biracial teenager in Colorado who contributes to a regular "Teen Talk" column for the internationally distributed magazine *New People*, described some of the frustrations of trying to counteract the stereotypes of biracial people perpetuated in the mass media. She wrote:

> *I received a call from the cable network Nickelodeon . . . and was interviewed for a program they wished to produce on biracial children. One of the first questions they asked me was what problems I had being biracial. When I told the interviewer that I could not remember any problems, she lost interest in me, and I was not used in the program. I was angry because if they only use biracial children with problems, what kind of message does that project? If all of the children used for these programs have problems, then people are going to expect that all biracial people have problems. That just strengthens the stereotype.*[1]

[72]

Maia noted that numerous other reporters for television shows, newspapers, and magazines have also assumed that because she is biracial she will have problems. She asked: "Why can't we let everyone know that biracial people are just like people of all other races? Why can't [the public] know we are normal?"[2]

Like Maia, others of mixed ancestry have asked similar questions and have struggled to point up the positive aspects of their interracial families. Leslie Lomax, past president of I-Pride, a multiracial family organization founded in San Francisco in 1979, said she has been called dozens of times by interviewers for talk shows to discuss issues surrounding families of mixed heritage. But Lomax, who is of mixed black/white heritage and a parent of a multiracial son, said she has learned from experience that radio and TV talk show hosts want to shock rather than truly educate the public about controversial issues. She declared emphatically:

> *Interviewers assume that there are numerous people who are "miserable" in their multicultural or interracial relationships or family situations. They even insist that children of mixed heritage have to have problems—like they know! I try to tell them that our I-Pride members are happy, healthy people—maybe even a bit boring they are so normal—but interviewers seldom listen to that. They have their own agenda, selling their show or newspapers or whatever. So I now tell interviewers that members of I-Pride are not interested in making fools of themselves or in being exploited on talk shows. None of us will appear on shows that thrive on sensationalism.*[3]

Similar reports come from other groups. Heidi McCue, program coordinator for the Interracial Connection family group in Williamsburg, Virginia, said she always tells producers of talk shows that members of her group are "normal people," but then producers "don't want our members to appear."[4]

In Georgia, a mother of two biracial children and director of another interracial organization, said that she, too, has received requests to appear on TV talk shows, but refuses the invitation unless hosts agree to ground rules. "I let them know in no uncertain terms that if they try to make a freak show out of us, I will get up and walk out—on camera!"[5]

Major newspaper and magazine articles also misrepresent and sometimes fabricate the negative, problematic nature of interracial families. Dickelle Fonda, a member of the Interracial Family Network in Evanston, Illinois, has been highly critical of a press that in her view presents a false image of how interracial families really function:

> . . . the majority of us are not spat upon or refused services in public, met with shock, disapproval and rejection by our families, subjected to offensive stares and comments, given guns as wedding gifts or terrorized by our neighbors. Nor do we live our lives in secret from our families or expect our children to visit their grandparents only in the dark of night in order to not offend the sensibilities of the neighbors. . . . To spotlight only such aberrant situations is an injustice to all interracial couples and our children, and continues to perpetuate the age-old mythology and negative stereotypes about our lives.[6]

A HISTORY OF NEGATIVE MEDIA IMAGES

Challenging negative media images of interracial couples and people of mixed ancestry is no easy task. Just as

U.S. society has regarded miscegenation as taboo, so have media images made it clear that even in the 1990s racial mixing is an explosive subject. Only a few films and TV dramas in recent years have shown interracial couples in any kind of favorable manner.

Since 1988, Mary Murchison-Edwords, director of the Interracial Club of Buffalo, New York, has been monitoring how films, dramatic TV programs, and videos portray interracial relationships. Her efforts began first as a way to provide information for members of her group, and then she began to share with other interracial family groups across the United States, a common practice for these organizations. She found that among the thousands of films and TV productions released since the days of silent films, only a few hundred have included the subject of interracial relationships.

When love relationships that crossed racial boundaries were depicted, seldom were the performers allowed to kiss, let alone take part in steamy sex scenes. In recent films with more candid sexual encounters, interracial relationships have been presented as torrid affairs or as love relationships doomed to heartache, despair, and eventual breakup or destruction.

For the most part, film characters involved in interracial relationships have been abandoned, exploited, ostracized by family and friends, subjected to racial hatred and violence, or driven to emotional turmoil or suicide because of their "forbidden" love. Usually the story line has called for the person of color involved in the relationship to be martyred or murdered. If performers have been people of color, they have been forced to play subservient roles: cooks, butlers, maids, mammies, fieldworkers, and so on.

In the past, many of the major characters representing African Americans, Native Americans, Asians, or Latinos have been portrayed by white performers in makeup and wigs. Murchison-Edwords pointed out that

[75]

numerous films also have perpetuated sexual myths, emphasizing "the rape of a White woman by a minority male"—black, Latin, and others—who have been "characterized as being obsessed with White women."[7] Black women regularly have been depicted as sex objects, prostitutes, or promiscuous Jezebels. Even into the 1990s, the myth that sex is the only component in an interracial relationship has prevailed.

One of the most controversial films in that genre was Spike Lee's *Jungle Fever*, which carried the explicit message that white women and black men sexually craved each other because of the taboo against interracial sex and that any children produced because of these lustful unions were "mixed nuts." While admiring Lee's talent and creativity, some critics of *Jungle Fever* said the film reflected Lee's own contempt for interracial relationships and reinforced the myths and lies about interracial families.

The negative stereotypes of people of mixed ancestry also have been passed on in other media. Among the common themes have been the identity crisis of the fictional character of mixed ancestry, a person's attempts to "pass" for white, and the supposedly disastrous discovery of the fictional character's nonwhite ancestry. In the opinion of Murchison-Edwords, the 1960 film *I Passed for White* "is one of the worst in regard to exploiting myths. It shows a light-skinned 'Negro' woman who marries a white man without revealing her mixed ancestry and later while expecting the birth of their first child agonizes over what color the baby's skin might be."

Murchison-Edwords is convinced that "film makers over the decades have not wanted to encourage racial mixing by presenting positive images of interracial couples and marriages. So they have continued showing us in a negative way, seldom if ever portraying how most of us conduct our lives."[8]

Yet Murchison-Edwords sees a "mini-trend" in which film and TV writers and producers have begun to present more representative examples of interracial relationships and multiracial people. Race and ethnicity are not used in the story lines to create conflicts that can only lead to tragic consequences.

A 1991 film *Mississippi Masala* is about an interracial relationship between a black man and Asian Indian woman in which color differences are not the issue for the couple, although family members feud over race and ethnicity. Filmmaker Mira Nair set out to portray a story that allows people to be human, "as opposed to conceiving of Asians and Africans as some anthropological other." Nair explained that "Masala literally means a collection of hot spices of different colors. . . . The whole film is a masala, really, because it involves several different countries, actors of three nations and clashing cultures." Yet the story recognizes that in spite of perceived differences between the black and brown communities, "there's a lot of commonality" in terms of "how important family and religion are."[9]

Several films, including *Mr. Baseball* and *Mistress*, released during the 1990s, presented interracial relationships as simply part of the story, not as a cause for conflict. In *The Bodyguard*, Whitney Houston plays a pop singer whose life has been threatened and Kevin Costner is the bodyguard hired to protect her. Their love relationship develops, but the conflict in the story has nothing to do with race.

Flirting is a coming-of-age story, focusing on two teenagers—an African girl from Uganda and an Australian boy—who meet in an Australian boarding school. Biracial actress Thandaway Adjewa, whose father is Ugandan and mother is of Kenyan and British ancestry, portrays an intelligent young woman who falls in love with a quick-witted young man. Although their lives are affected by the turmoil in Uganda, the teenagers relate to each other in a healthy manner, interacting without regard to color differences and with concern about who they are as thinking, caring people.

TV soap operas have followed a pattern similar to that of film, steering clear of interracial romances or even the suggestion of a possible sexual attraction of a white person with someone of color. As recently as the late 1980s, when an interracial relationship was depicted, the pair seldom became sexually involved let alone married; just the suggestion of marriage would bring protests from viewers and network officials. Usually, soap opera story lines have called for interracial couples to break up, leave town, die, or in some way disappear from the script and show. In the early 1990s, however, a few soap opera stories that included people of mixed ancestry or interracial couples began to move away from racial divisions to center more on such life issues as the consequences of divorce and remarriage, child custody battles, adoption, and the abuse of economic and political power.

"HIDDEN" HERITAGE?

Many people applaud the kinds of media presentations that refrain from presenting color and culture differences as major life conflicts. But a few entertainment reviewers wonder why the mixed ancestry of celebrities is not acknowledged and celebrated. Many dozens, if not hundreds of prominent people—TV personalities, entertainers, sports figures, models, politicians, and others—are of multiracial heritage. As a general rule, though, these celebrities have been silent about their backgrounds or, as a matter of choice or because of political pressure, have identified with one ancestry.

Some celebrities of mixed lineage have "passed" for white. Usually they have hidden their mixed ancestry because of discrimination in American society and because their careers would have been limited if the nonwhite part of their heritage had been revealed.

Certainly the print and electronic media over the years have for the most part categorized famous people by their nonwhite ancestry, no matter what the hue of their skin. A recent political example is Hazel O'Leary, head of the U.S. Department of Energy. The media have consistently labeled her a black member of President Bill Clinton's cabinet, but there is little doubt that she is of mixed-race heritage.

However, just as there is a "mini-trend" toward portraying more "normal," real-life interracial families and couples in films and TV shows, so there is a somewhat more open discussion today of mixed ancestry among media celebrities. Some observers believe such public disclosure helps provide positive role models for multiracial young people. Kevin Costner, for example, has proudly claimed his part-Indian heritage and his honorary membership in a tribe of the Sioux Nation. Celebrities Dolly Parton, Loretta Lynn, James Garner, Burt Reynolds, and Johnny Cash are among those who are recognized as having part Cherokee ancestry.

Amerasians such as award-winning playwright Velina Hasu Houston and actress Mariko Tse have touted their mixed ancestry as a positive, though sometimes frustrating, heritage. Nobel Prize-winning poet Derek Walcott of African, Dutch, and English ancestry, who was born in the Caribbean, celebrates his mixed heritage in the language and imagery he uses. Singer Mariah Carey, whose father is of black, white, and Latino (Venezuelan) ancestry and mother is of Irish parentage, has proclaimed her multiracial background many times. Ironically, however, she was first criticized in the black community for being a "white girl trying to sing black." Later, after Carey publicly pointed out her black heritage, she was praised as a gifted, black musician, but never recognized as a talented, mixed-race individual.

Actor Giancarlo Esposito of Italian and African American ancestry, who has played roles in several Spike Lee films, said he identifies himself as an African American because that is what U.S. society dictates. But he considers himself as "an individual first" and is frustrated by the stereotyped views of multiracial people and interracial relationships. In fact, in an interview for *New People* magazine, he criticized his friend Spike Lee's film *Jungle Fever* as a story depicting not a true human relationship but rather one that "just furthered existing stereotypes. It didn't do us any good."[10]

In Esposito's view, society has problems with interracial relationships and children of mixed ancestry because there is a fear of "diluting" a particular race and a "real fear of a multicultural world." But he believes that ultimately love will win out and help break down racial barriers not only in the media but in American society as well.[11]

CHAPTER SEVEN

MULTIRACIAL PEOPLE IN OTHER NATIONS

A group of teenagers at a youth camp [in Thailand] drag a reluctant Amerasian girl up to a counselor, saying, "She's a foreigner's child—look at her hair!" and making the girl remove her cap under which she had carefully tucked her long blond tresses.

—an incident witnessed and described by Jan Robyn Weisman in "'Half Children': A History of Racial Mixing and Racially Mixed Individuals in Thailand," included in Interracial Identity: Celebration, Conflict, or Choice, p. 35

"The much-vaunted U.S. ideal of the 'melting pot' has been a living reality in Latin America for centuries (and also the Middle East, Southeast Asia, Polynesia and even parts of Spain)," wrote Carlos Fernandez, a San Francisco attorney and one of the founders of the Association of MultiEthnic Americans (AMEA), a multiracial organization. "In Mexico and the Andean region, the Native American component tends to predominate; in the Caribbean and Brazil, African ancestry is shared by many. Take a look at the faces of one of the fastest-growing ethnic groups in [the United States] the so-called 'Hispanics,' and you will see something of the faces of the future."[1]

Although some regions of the world may have achieved the "melting pot" ideal, as Hernandez suggested, there is little doubt that in some nations racially mixed people are still considered a threat to the social structure. It is impossible here to present a comprehensive look at how people of mixed ancestry are treated and fare worldwide. But certainly, as is evident from the brief examples that follow, ethnocentric beliefs are prevalent in many nations, and those views have sometimes led to prejudice and discrimination against if not outright ostracism of racially mixed people.

SOUTH AFRICA'S SYSTEM

One notorious example is the apartheid system in South Africa where a small white minority of primarily Dutch and British heritage separated from and suppressed vast numbers of nonwhite groups. In 1950, the white-controlled South African government passed a basic law that established apartheid by classifying everyone at birth according to racial "population groups." The government categorized people of color as Black (African), Asian, or Colored (people of mixed race who are primarily descendants of European settlers, African natives, and Asian slaves).

Coloreds have always had more privileges than Blacks in terms of housing and jobs in South Africa. Yet thousands of Coloreds like millions of Blacks were forcibly removed from their homes in areas that were too close for whites to tolerate. These lands were then classified for "whites only."

As Coloreds began to side with Blacks in anti-apartheid struggles, the government tried to win them over by granting voting rights in 1983. But over the years, there were numerous conflicts between Colored groups and Black groups, and many Coloreds feared that Blacks would take over their jobs. When Nelson Mandela, a Black leader who was imprisoned for twenty-five years, was released in 1990, political campaigns got under way to elect him president of South Africa, and Coloreds at first supported him. But over the next four years, Coloreds became even more fearful that Blacks would be an economic threat, so the vast majority turned to the white-dominated National Party.

In 1994, after years of pressure from the international community as well as from within the country, a historic election took place. For the first time Blacks were able to vote, and they helped elect Nelson Mandela president of South Africa. U.S. president Bill Clinton in a radio address following the election said "the miracle of South Africa's rebirth as a nonracial democracy is an inspiring testament to the courage and vision of its citizens." Yet the country has a long way to go in reconciling militants on both sides of the apartheid issue and in integrating all of the color factions.

EUROPEAN VIEWS ON RACIAL
AND ETHNIC MIXING

European countries have extensive histories of distinguishing people in terms of their racial or ethnic heritage. And in recent years attacks against people who are not part of the dominant white European group have been on the rise in Germany, France, and England. In Eastern Europe, Serbians within the territory once known as Yugoslavia have grabbed land and killed or pushed out people for so-called ethnic-cleansing purposes—to establish the area for what the Serbians call their own kind, although many being forced out are of similar heritage as the Serbs.

For many Europeans, one of the most frightening trends of recent years is the rise of hate crimes against foreigners or those thought to be foreigners. Refugees seeking asylum from war and political oppression and immigrants looking for jobs are blamed for the economic and social problems that plague many European countries. As a result, neo-Nazis (new Nazis), or skinheads (so named because of their shaved heads), and other racist groups have instigated thousands of violent incidents against people who appear different from white Europeans.

The neo-Nazis and other white supremacists revere the former Nazi dictator Adolf Hitler, who rose to power in the 1930s and killed himself as World War II came to a close. Hitler believed in a "superior" race of "pure" gentile Germans. He maintained that German "purity" had to be protected from Jews and others whom he called "inferior." During World War II, Hitler and his Nazi Party were responsible for the Holocaust—the mass murder of millions of Jews, Gypsies (a nomadic people of mixed ancestry perhaps originating in India), Poles, and many others labeled "undesirable."

Since the end of World War II, racist groups have been organizing in Europe, and during the late 1980s, European neo-Nazis organized vicious attacks against people from other parts of the world, as well as European Jews. Thousands of attacks have been reported in Germany since the former communist East Germany united with West Germany in October 1990. According to a news report, "the first major outbreak of anti-foreigner violence occurred September 18, 1991, when neo-Nazi skinheads attacked Vietnamese guest workers in the eastern German city of Hoyerswerda."[2]

During 1992, an estimated 2,000 attacks were reported, among them firebombings of homes and hostels for refugees, and attacks against handicapped people and against Jews and Jewish cemeteries and Holocaust memorials. The long-established Turkish community, separated from the white majority, also came under attack. A Turkish woman and two young children were killed and several Turks were injured in a firebombing in November 1992. That same month a traveling businessman—a German gentile—was beaten to death because his attackers mistakenly thought he was a Jew. Teenagers beat and partially blinded an African man and accosted and kicked a teenage girl they thought was a foreigner.[3]

The following month, Hartho Tonino Roseno, of German and Indonesian heritage, reported that many dark-skinned Germans fear neo-Nazi violence. He expressed fear for his own life since he once was beaten by three neo-Nazis. Roseno said that because of his part-Asian heritage he is made to feel out of place in his own land. In his view, the racist groups are not the only Germans with such ideas—he believes the problem is widespread.[4]

Indeed, several reports have indicated that one out of every three Germans surveyed in a national poll believes that the Nazi era provided some benefits for Germans. At least 14 percent of those surveyed agreed with the statement that "It is the Jews' own fault that they have been persecuted so often in their history."[5]

On the other hand, news reports have indicated that tens of thousands of Germans have taken part in rallies across the nation to protest and demand action to reduce anti-Semitic and racist violence. Nevertheless, attacks against "strangers" go on and have been reported in other nations such as France, Britain, the Netherlands, and Spain, and numerous people of mixed ancestry in Europe share the fears of Roseno. They also must deal with labeling in much the same way that Americans of mixed ancestry do, although the categories for people of color vary.

In England, for example, people of color—whether from the Caribbean, Pakistan, India, Sri Lanka, or other part of the world—are categorized as "black." So how does this affect British citizens of mixed heritage? British authors Yasmin Alibhai Brown and Anne Montague explored this question in interviews with biracial or multiracial children and their parents for a book titled *The Colour of Love*, published in 1992. Excerpts from some of their interviews appeared in the magazine *New Statesman & Society*.

In one case, Denise Seneviratne, whose father is Sri Lankan and mother is French and Jewish, said her father "wanted to be British and that meant white British. So we always lived in very white areas." As a result the family lost all contact with Asians, and they seldom acknowledged publicly any affiliation with Jews because of fears that they would not be accepted. Yet Denise knew from an early age that she was not perceived as "white" even though she felt "white with a brown skin." She said, "I looked Asian" and "Asian kids used to walk up to me and try to speak to me in one of the languages. I would be so embarrassed because I couldn't communicate with them and wasn't part of them and didn't want to be." Denise reported that she was always seen as "black in the eyes of other people. I always had racist abuse thrown at me."

Denise could not discuss racism or other conflicts with her parents because of their denial about their own heritage and intermixture. But today she no longer feels like an outsider and believes that she is part of a culture of mixed-race people like herself. "We are perhaps the children of the future—not having a strong addiction to one culture, but being a mixture," she said.[6]

BEING "DIFFERENT" IN JAPAN

In many Asian countries where so-called racial and cultural purity have long been prized, people generally are expected to fit not only a biological mold but also a particular pattern of behavior. People who vary in any way may encounter prejudicial barriers. To the Japanese, for example, being "different" is in many cases tantamount to being a troublemaker. Most people conform to society's rules and customs. If not, as the saying goes, "*Deru kugi wa utareru*" ("The protruding nail gets hammered down").

Nonconformists may suffer harassment or discrimination, which has been the case in the educational system. Students who are above-average in intelligence, have physical or mental disabilities, or who simply lack interest in team sports may be labeled "different" and therefore subject to "hammering." Or the person who is "different" may be of mixed ancestry, as was the case of a fifteen-year-old boy whose mother is white American and father is Japanese.

Because the teenager corrected his teacher's English

grammar and, in the teacher's words, was "going beyond the curriculum and advancing too fast," he received a failing grade. His "fast advancement" along with his obvious mixed ancestry brought taunts from classmates who daily took up the chant "Stinking foreigner! Your mother is an American so you must have AIDS!" School officials suggested that the boy be placed in a school for foreigners in spite of the fact that he was born in Japan, is a Japanese citizen, and speaks fluent Japanese.

The demand for conformity in Japan has led to a brutal form of bullying among junior and senior high school students. Known as *ijime*, the bullying is ongoing and can escalate to physical attacks on Japanese students who their peers decide are nonconformists. Although Japanese school authorities say that *ijime* incidents have been dropping, bullying caused 300 students to commit suicide in 1992, and that same year Japanese public schools reported 4,854 physical attacks and thirteen deaths, nearly all related to bullying.

A teenage girl was systematically taunted and finally attacked and killed because she "dressed poorly" in school uniforms that had been handed down from her older sister. One of the girl's assailants said wearing a used uniform was an "irritation" to "all other students [who] have new uniforms each year."

In January 1993, Yuhei Kodama, a thirteen-year-old student who had long been a bullying target, was beaten while in the gym of the junior high school he attended. He was bound in a wrestling mat and smothered to death. His "crime"? He was considered "bookish" and poor at team sports. According to a news report from Tokyo, "He was clever with words, and would ask questions in class, showing a streak of individualism that stuck out like the proverbial protruding nail in an educational system where the scores—not initiative, creative thinking or inquiry—are the sole standard of academic success."[7]

[88]

Not all people who are considered different in Japan or other Asian countries are subject to such vicious abuse. Teresa Williams, a young woman of European and Japanese descent living in California, noted that whenever she and her brother have visited Japan (where they grew up), they have been treated like foreigners until people heard their unaccented Japanese.

"As if a lightbulb goes on in their heads, Japanese people immediately respond by asking, 'Haafu desho? (You're 'half,' aren't you?)'. . . [There's] instant recognition of our blended heritage," Williams explained, adding that some Japanese "relish us for our exoticism" while others "despise us" because "our [Japanese] mother married a measly U.S. serviceman and not a business man or a man of [high status]." In Williams's view, "The Japanese are more subtle and polite [than Americans] about their prejudicial attitudes." Since she and her brother are "caught in the midst," they have learned to get along, she reported.[8]

THE PLIGHT OF AMERASIANS

Among the tens of thousands of mixed offspring in Asian countries, most are progeny of U.S. servicemen who were stationed at military bases in Korea, Vietnam, Thailand, Cambodia, Laos, and the Philippines during the U.S. military buildup and wars in Korea and Vietnam. During the Vietnam era alone (1962–1975), tens of thousands of children of American servicemen and Vietnamese women were born. Known as Amerasians, many have become adults, but some 30,000 children were left behind when American troops pulled out of Vietnam in 1975.[9]

The majority of Amerasians have been subjected to taunts and name-calling abuse. Many have been labeled bui doi, the "dust of life," by Vietnamese who are part of a relatively homogeneous (unmixed) society. They frequently are shunned because they are fatherless. Few have received more than an elementary education, since financial need has forced them to find jobs, usually menial labor, or they have lived as "street people" for years, begging for money and food.

Except for an occasional news story, Americans for more than a decade generally ignored the plight of Amerasians in Vietnam and other Asian countries. Few servicemen acknowledged their paternity, sometimes because they did not know about their offspring. In many cases, however, accepting responsibility for children would not have been condoned, because of the long-held notion in the United States that interracial sex is acceptable but not permanent interracial relationships.

However, in 1982, the U.S. Congress passed the Amerasian Act, which allowed Amerasians to emigrate to the United States under the Orderly Departure Program of the United Nations (UN). The UN program was originally designed to handle "boat people," refugees from Asian countries who risked their lives in flimsy sea craft to flee Communist rule. But relations between Vietnam and the United States deteriorated, and emigration halted for a time.

In 1987, the U.S. Congress passed legislation known as the Amerasian Homecoming Act, which has since been amended and allows not just Amerasian children but also adults (the average Amerasian is over eighteen years old) to immigrate with their families. However, Amerasians from Vietnam do not get along as well in U.S. society as, for example, those of mixed Japanese and American heritage, according to research conducted by Kieu-Linh Caroline Valverde, cofounder of the Multiracial Asian International Network. In her view, Amerasians from Vietnam generally

> *. . . do not have family support systems or the*
> *understanding of U.S. culture. . . . All their lives,*
> *Amerasians have been defined by society at*
> *large. One moment they are told that they are*
> *as worthless as dust, and the next they are told*
> *that they are precious as gold [because they*
> *have] a chance to go to America. However,*
> *crossing the Pacific does not mean escaping*
> *labels and stereotypes. Voluntary agencies, the*
> *Vietnamese American community, and the main-*
> *stream community all have preconceived ideas*
> *about Amerasians.* [10]

By contrast, the French, who had earlier fought the Vietnamese and were defeated, withdrew all their troops and brought to France an estimated 25,000 children of French and Vietnamese ancestry, known as Eurasians. In France, Eurasians were provided with educational opportunities, were able to gain citizenship at age eighteen, and some were able to bring their Vietnamese mothers to France.

Certainly the Vietnamese Amerasians are not the only people of mixed ancestry to encounter problems. A U.S. military buildup also took place in Thailand during the Vietnam war, and an estimated 8,000 or more children of mixed ancestry were born between 1962 and 1975. Jan Robyn Weisman, a Californian of mixed ancestry and a former Peace Corps volunteer in Thailand, has sponsored a Thai child and has returned often to Thailand for research and to serve as an interpreter. Her studies and personal experiences have shown that Thai society is more heterogeneous—made up of more dissimilar people—than other Asian countries. Although Thais do not exhibit hostility toward Americans, they do stigmatize children born out of wedlock, and many children of mixed heritage in Thailand fit that category.

If the children are easily recognized by appearance as being mixed (light hair and freckles or skin tones of darker hue than Thais), they may be taunted and suffer discrimination, particularly if they happen to be of part–African American descent. Weisman, citing an example from her own experience while visiting an orphanage in Thailand where several Amerasian children lived, wanted to know "why a half-Black child [would] be singing pop music rather than playing an instrument in a classical orchestra." The social worker explained that "the children who play the traditional instruments have to be light-skinned in order for it to look pretty on stage."[11]

Amerasians in the Philippines are one more group forsaken by American servicemen. Beginning in 1898, when the United States seized the Philippines from Spain, the U.S. military maintained bases in the Philippines—even after the Philippines became independent in 1946—as part of a Mutual Defense Treaty. But because of Philippine opposition to the U.S. military bases and less need for such defense, most of the U.S. military has pulled out. That last base, the Subic Bay Naval Station, closed in 1992. However, because of the long U.S. military presence, an estimated 50,000 people of part-Filipino and part-American descent, including about 3,500 children under the age of eighteen, are now part of the Philippine population.

Although people of mixed heritage in the Philippines do not suffer the kind of discrimination that has been reported in other Asian countries, many children of Filipino and American ancestry have been abandoned. They are not eligible for U.S. citizenship unless American fathers are willing to affirm paternity, which few have acknowledged. Amerasians in the Philippines were excluded from the U.S. law that allows others of Asian and American ancestry to enter the United States and become citizens.

Apparently this exclusion came about because lawmakers assumed racially mixed people would be tolerated better in the Philippines than elsewhere. Nevertheless, a lawsuit on behalf of the "throwaway" children in the Philippines was initiated in the United States in the spring of 1993. The legal maneuver, which will probably take years to settle, is designed to force the U.S. Navy and federal government to acknowledge some responsibility for the children. And President Fidel Ramos of the Philippines declared that his country, too, should share in that responsibility.

CHAPTER EIGHT

"CHANGE AGENTS," FACILITATORS, AND MEDIATORS

Many years ago, my baby daughter (who is multiracial) and I were grocery shopping. An obnoxious . . . man walked up to us and began making extremely ugly comments, and asking what I was doing with that child! . . . My little daughter, who was very friendly and not yet three, did not perceive his hatred. She didn't understand the meaning of what he was saying—and she started a conversation with him! She told him that we were going on a picnic, and that we were here to buy some chicken. Did he like chicken? "Picnics are fun. We have a dog at our house, and I like to play with her. Do you have a dog at your house?" She had no hostility.

My baby ended up engaging that man in a five-minute conversation. . . . I stood there, amazed and unbelieving. I'll never forget the look on that

man's face as he walked away from us. It was
questioning and confused. He had learned some-
thing—and he had changed.
>   *—Linda Thomas, I-Pride*
>   *member (September 1992)*

Although people worldwide develop negative attitudes toward and discrimination against people who appear different from themselves, groups and individuals in many parts of the world work to counteract racism and prevent discrimination. In the United States, these "change agents," facilitators, or mediators also attempt to dismantle some of the myths about multiracial people.

"The only way you're going to make a change is to keep talking about things and get people to think about what's right. . . . I know that people of different races can live together in peace because we do it in my house," declared biracial teenager Brian Harris of southern California. "If people would just . . . treat everyone else with respect, a lot of our problems would disappear. It's hard enough to have good relationships without creating all sorts of additional barriers."[1]

Brian and his parents are members of an interracial family group called A Place for Us with headquarters in Gardena, California. The group and Brian's parents have supported the teenager's efforts to solicit appearances on TV and radio talk shows and to speak before civic groups and at high school and college forums. During his appearances he points out that children are born "color-blind," and he blames adults for teaching youngsters to be prejudiced. America's cultural and racial diversity should be celebrated rather than condemned, he insists.

In early 1993, Brian announced on a network TV show that he had formed an international pen-pal club called Friendship Sees No Color (later renamed Alliance Beyond Color) "to promote understanding among the races." Within a few months he had received over 5,000 responses from both young people and adults who wanted to get to know people of other racial backgrounds through his letter-writing campaign.[2]

SPREADING THE WORD

Young people and adults of mixed heritage across the United States are trying to educate the public about the damaging effects of belittling another person because of the color of her or his skin or because of a multiracial ancestry. They often emphasize the advantages of being of mixed heritage and being able to identify with more than one culture, sometimes learning another language. However, they also discuss some of the problems that biracial people face.

A common problem, often expressed by interviewees for this book, is the peer pressure to choose a single racial identity in order to be accepted by African-American, white, Latino, Asian, or whatever group. But an increasing number of biracial people are refusing to accept a single category for identification. As Maya Reyes, a student at Berkeley High School, noted: "I consider myself 'Blaxican' because I am Black and Mexican."[3]

Being able to openly discuss the issues of mixed heritage is a step forward in recognizing that racial as well as ethnic blending continually takes place and has been going on for thousands of years. "Public forums and multiracial support groups have given interracial families and people of mixed ancestry a sense of identity and a voice," said AMEA president Ramona Douglass. She has been able over the past decade to get her message across by speaking to civic groups and professional organizations, stressing pride in her identity and the need to have her blended ancestry acknowledged. As she explained:

> I've gone toe-to-toe with African-American social workers and clinicians who frequently bring their own value system into therapy when counseling children of part black heritage. Their assumption is that these children are having problems because of their mixture. Children are counseled to identify as black—no matter what. That is simply wrong for many biracial or multiracial people. I believe people such as myself have the right and duty to make their own decisions about their identity. I consider myself a woman of color—I'm the daughter of an Italian mother and a father who is part black and part Sioux. All of those heritages are part of me.[4]

Douglass added that she believes many biracial and multiracial people are now "holding their ground and showing the world that they are not confused about who they are. We are becoming more active in trying to influence the nation's attitudes about race and racial/ethnic categories," she said.[5]

Other multiracial people and interracial families have produced documentary-type TV shows, films, radio programs, and nonfiction books that provide a realistic view of multicultural families and people of mixed ancestry. Newsletters published by multiracial organizations and distributed to commercial media as well as to members are another way to highlight the positive aspects of racially and ethnically blended families.

National and regional conferences and forums that are covered by the media also call attention to the positive aspects of multiracial families and the way individuals deal with society's stereotypes of multiracial people. Multiracial organizations, which have formed across the United States (see Appendix for names and addresses), sponsor most of these public events. For example, during October each year, which is cultural diversity month in California, Multiracial Americans of Southern California (MASC) sponsors Kaleidoscope, a one-day conference that celebrates interracial families and multiracial people as well as cultural diversity. The conference provides seminars on such topics as interracial dating, multiethnic identity, transracial adoption, multiracial parenting, and dealing with daily racism.

A special commemorative conference sponsored by the Interracial Family Circle (IFC) of Washington, D.C., in June 1992 brought together more than 200 interracial families from across the United States. The conference marked the twenty-fifth anniversary of the 1967 landmark U.S. Supreme Court decision (*Loving* v. *Virginia*) that abolished all sixteen remaining state laws prohibiting interracial marriages. Along with attending workshops, participants honored the Loving family: Mildred Loving of African-American and Native-American ancestry and her late husband, Richard, of white ancestry (who died in a car accident in 1975) and their children and grandchildren.

Three generations of the multiracial Loving family attended the conference, dramatically demonstrating by their very existence that love and determination can help people overcome barriers to racial harmony. Conference participants heard the Lovings' story as told by the couple's lawyers, and now friends of long standing, who defended them.

In 1958, Mildred Jeter and Richard Loving were known as quiet, unassuming people with no interest in social activism. They had both grown up in Virginia's rural hill country, fallen in love, and like many other couples planned to marry. Although they were unaware of Virginia's law that criminalized interracial marriage, they went to Washington, D.C., for their vows, because the district did not require a waiting period before the ceremony could take place. When the Lovings returned to Virginia, they were soon arrested for breaking the antimiscegenation law, even though their marriage was legally performed. A county sheriff roused the Lovings from their sleep at 2:00 A.M. one morning and took them to the Bowling Green jail. Later, each was sentenced to a one-year prison term, but the judge suspended the sentences on the condition that the couple leave Virginia and not return for twenty-five years.

The Lovings moved to Washington, D.C., where they lived with relatives for several years. But Mildred Loving wrote to then U.S. attorney general Robert F. Kennedy for help. Kennedy turned the case over to Bernard S. Cohen, a young American Civil Liberties Union lawyer, and Phillip Hirschkop, who was just out of law school and had been hired by Cohen. The two appealed the Lovings' case to the state supreme court and lost. But their appeal to the U.S. Supreme Court resulted in the High Court's June 12, 1967, decision, which held that the Virginia law prohibiting interracial marriage violated the Fourteenth Amendment of the U.S. Constitution.

STUDENT GROUPS

The effects of the High Court decision went far beyond the Loving family, of course, and paved the way for many others to legally marry across racial lines. As Joan Walsh, in a 1992 article for the *San Francisco Chronicle's Sunday Image* magazine noted: "demagogues preach race hatred," but Americans are "mixing more and more." In her own neighborhood, Walsh "made a mental tally of the mixed-race families around [her]: the Latino-Anglo couple three doors down; the Chinese-Jewish family across the street; my Iranian-Muslim/Jewish friends, expecting their first child; another friend's African/Canadian-Jewish daughter who attends a Spanish-language school in San Francisco."[6]

Because of the increasing number of multiracial families in California in particular and in the nation in general, high school and college students who are of mixed parentage have been forming activist groups. They meet on a regular basis to discuss ways to address the needs of people of mixed ancestry, including how to deal with the pressure to identify with a particular group, which can be frustrating and stressful. A Stanford (California) student of mixed ancestry explained, "When I got to Stanford, I didn't think of myself as black or Korean or white. I thought of myself as Carl Hicks. But everyone kept labeling me."[7]

Hicks was determined to identify himself rather than allow others to do so. Along with other students of mixed parentage who shared his views, he organized Spectrum in 1990. Within the group, individuals of mixed ancestry can socialize without being placed on the defensive or being judged by their physical appearance. That same year at Stanford, a group of women of Asian and white heritage formed the Half Asian People's Association, or HAPA, the Hawaiian term for a person of mixed ancestry.

Students of mixed heritage have organized groups on many other college campuses, including New York University, Harvard, the University of Michigan, Kansas State, the University of California at Berkeley and at Los Angeles. At Berkeley, there are two multiracial organizations: the Multiethnic Interracial Student's Coalition (MISC) and the Hapa Issues Forum (HIF), which addresses the issues that arise for people of part-

Japanese ancestry and their relationship to the Japanese American community.

Japanese Americans, who number about 800,000 according to the most recent census data, marry people of other racial groups at a much higher rate than other Asians. As a result, each year since 1982 Japanese-white births have outnumbered Japanese-Japanese births. This means that in the future "Hapas will become the most numerous portion of the Japanese American community . . . [and] by the dawn of the twenty-first century, the typical Japanese American will be a Hapa," according to HIF, which hopes to broaden the definition of the Japanese American. "To remain a viable community, Japanese Americans must accept the reality of the changing dynamics. . . . Without meaningful participation of Hapas . . . the Japanese community faces extinction," HIF leaders stated.[8]

At Berkeley High School, Vasey Tao McClory, who described herself as "half-Chinese and half-white," helped found what is believed to be the first group of multiracial high school students, the Interracial Students Union (ISU). Although the school is considered one of the most integrated high schools in the United States, "when you look around you see that people are really segregated with separate associations for Asians, blacks, Hispanics, or whatever," McClory said. "Our group [ISU] is one of the only places where students of mixed heritage can get together to share different racial experiences. We hope to reach out to more people," she said, and by doing so make the public more aware of what it means to be of mixed ancestry and truly integrated.[9]

To develop public awareness of issues that concern people of mixed heritage, student and family groups are developing information centers with books, films, and articles about multiracial people and to sponsor lectures and forums. In 1993, for example, members of ISU, HIF, and MISC were part of a public forum called "Into the Mix" held on the University of California Berkeley campus. The nine panelists discussed their experiences growing up and developing their own identities as people of mixed racial descent; they also described their strategies for living successfully in a diverse but racist society that insists on categorizing people by physical appearance and culture.

Saman Dashti, whose father is Iranian and mother is Haitian, said "When I was growing up in New York in a diverse neighborhood there was so much hell to deal with that being mixed was hardly a problem. Being mixed wasn't an issue until I went to an all-boys, primarily white, Catholic high school. I didn't bond very well with groups at the school, so I usually found a humorous way to deal with racial issues—humor was my weapon and my shield. I just didn't deal with race and questions about my mixed heritage. Then I came to UC Berkeley, and I found that people considered racial issues seriously. Now I'm trying to learn ways to break down barriers because of race."[10]

MEDIATORS

New Yorker Charles Byrd of black, white, and Native American ancestry and publisher/editor of *Interracial Classified*, believes that one way to break down racial barriers is for people of mixed heritage to volunteer to be mediators or facilitators whenever there are racial conflicts in a community. In Byrd's view, "Mixed-race people could demonstrate that there are alternatives to playing the 'race' game." He envisions a national board of "multiracial mediators, on twenty-four-hour call, willing and prepared to dash out in the middle of the night to help extinguish a newly started race fire

. . . trained to reduce the emotional charge inherent in any such conflict, preventing it from escalating into full-blown race riots. . . . Akin to an impartial, third-party labor mediation and arbitration board, this group would be a more aggressively 'hands-on' national mixed-race version of the newly established Independent Commission on Human Relations in New York City."[11]

Byrd said he would like to see the Association of MultiEthnic Americans play that role on a national level, acting as a watchdog agency and initiating local responses when necessary. "Why couldn't AMEA fax Associated Press and other media contacts the names of local multicultural groups that could send emissaries to mediate when a conflict arises, people who understand both sides of racial issues to talk about ways to relieve tension? Why do officials always summon someone like Jesse Jackson?" he asked rhetorically.[12]

However, AMEA is not likely to serve as a mediator group anytime soon, if ever, since most efforts of the organization are geared toward convincing the U.S. Census Bureau to establish a multiracial category for the next national census (a topic covered in the next chapter). But individuals and local multiracial organizations do sometimes serve as mediators or are forced into the role. For example, a crew from MASC was able to serve in a type of mediation capacity after the 1992 riots in Los Angeles by helping to clean up the streets and by discussing how one group knocking another group can hurt multiracial families in very personal ways.

Mediation before violence breaks out sometimes "can be very informal," said one high school student of mixed parentage, "like just letting groups in conflict know that I can look at some issues from two different viewpoints. At least that gets some kids to see what it's like to be in somebody else's shoes for a change. Another thing, I think it's important when you're in a group that's hitting on people of another race—like blacks or Asians running down white people—to say, 'Hey, cool it. You're stereotyping a part of me!'"[13]

Other young people and adults of mixed heritage have helped conduct sensitivity or walk-in-my-shoes workshops for those who have had little contact with anyone outside their own racial group. In effective mediation discussions, people need to be able to speak openly about their experiences and feelings. As one student said, "I can't understand why someone thinks it's okay to call me a 'nigger jap.' I'm proud of the ancestries of both my parents, and I'm a decent person. Why do people think they have the right to offend me with such slurs?"[14]

EDUCATIONAL PROGRAMS

In recent years college and university classes have begun to address interracial subjects in a formal, academic manner. "People of Mixed Racial Descent," thought to be the first course to explore the subject of multiracial people, was launched in 1980 at UC Berkeley by Terry Wilson, professor of Native American Studies. He initiated the class because he wanted to emphasize the advantages of being a multiracial and multicultural person, providing constructive portrayals of multiracial people rather than passing on the negative images that have come from academic studies, literature, and films of the past. Wilson has little patience with the "gospel of social science," which long has theorized that people of mixed ancestry are "marginal." As a person of Potawatomi and French-Canadian ancestry, "I ain't no marginal man!" he said emphatically. During his course, Wilson often tells about his own life experiences, and his teaching is based on the premise that "students learn and remember if a human being talks to them, and if that human being is not afraid to communicate his or her experiences as a means to explain what life is really about, rather than depending on artificial constructs and theories developed by sociologists." Thus he requires students in his class to research a variety of topics related to people of mixed racial descent and to present their findings orally before turning in formal papers.[15]

When Wilson began his course, only a couple of dozen students enrolled, but enrollment has grown steadily and dramatically each year. During the fall 1992 semester, he had to turn away about five hundred students who wanted to sign up for the class. Several of Wilson's colleagues are teaching similar undergraduate seminars at UC Santa Cruz and UC Los Angeles. Other universities across the nation are considering such classes also.

It seems logical that a person of mixed heritage should be able to say freely, as Vasey Tao McClory of California does: "Some days I call myself 'Asian-white' and other days I become 'white-Asian.' It really doesn't matter which order. I cherish both of my racial backgrounds."[16]

Yet McClory, like many others of mixed heritage, knows that there is still a long way to go before people's blended ancestries are officially acknowledged by institutions such as schools and government and informally accepted by Americans with a penchant for cataloging and classifying.

CHAPTER NINE

AN "EMERGING POPULATION"

*If I could talk to the president of the United States
I would tell him that we should be able to have
our dream. We should be able to mark multiracial on forms.*

> —an eight-year-old biracial
> boy of Atlanta, Georgia

Any student who has applied for a magnet school program or taken achievement and college admission tests
and anyone who has completed a U.S. census form or
perhaps a social security or hospital admittance form is
familiar with the check-off list for racial or ethnic classification. It begins with the basic instruction: "Please
select one." In most states, parents are also asked to
mark a single racial or ethnic category for their children when enrolling them in school. For many people of
mixed heritage and parents of biracial children, being

[106]

forced to choose just one classification can be insulting, since checking a single box denies the basic heritage of the children.

Kent Syverud, a law professor at the University of Michigan, noted in 1990 after completing his form for the U.S. census with its check-off list for racial or ethnic classification:

> *We dutifully blackened the little circles to indicate that . . . my wife is female and Chinese, and that I am male and white. Next came the [questions about dependent children]. . . . Question 4 asked us to state the race that each of our sons "considers himself to be." The choices included "White," "Black," "American Indian," "Chinese," "Japanese," "Other Asian or Pacific Islander," and, finally, "Other Race". . . . What a ridiculous question. When I ask my 4-year-old what race he considers himself to be, he is most likely to answer "pirate." (He's been into Peter Pan lately.) . . . Exasperated, we asked our kids what race they considered themselves to be. Our 2-year-old's answer, which we inserted in the box marked "Other Race" was "American."*[1]

THE CATEGORY DEBATE

The "Other Race" category on the U.S. census form was included in 1970 as an attempt by the federal government to count the number of people of multiracial parentage. People marking the "other" box also have written in their diverse ethnic backgrounds, even though the U.S. Census Bureau has counted only the first racial or ethnic classification listed. Many, however, would agree with biracial teenager Roland Hill of

St. Louis, Missouri, who said simply: "I don't feel like an *other.*"[2]

Multiracial people are often told to pick a category with which they most identify. If they do not, someone else usually makes that choice for them, which has been the case for multiracial teenager Carlo Adams of California whose mother is from El Salvador and father is from Belize. Because his skin is dark like his father's, Adams is considered black but he thinks of himself as Latino. "I speak the language, I grew up with the culture, I listen to the music, but all my life I haven't been considered Hispanic because I look black. . . . In the house I'm more Hispanic, but outside, I'm black."[3]

Bryan Pozzo, a student at UC Berkeley who is of Mexican, Italian, and Welsh descent, said he identified himself as Mexican when he completed tests for college application because "It's a minority, and colleges are trying to increase minority enrollment, so I figured I'd have a better shot at getting in." But Pozzo explained to a news reporter that selecting this category did not mean he ignored the other part of his heritage. "When I think of myself, I don't think of myself as one or the other—I'm me," he said.[4]

UCLA professor G. Reginald Daniel, of multiracial heritage, well understands the importance of numbers in assessing needs and determining how people of color are progressing economically and socially. But he would like to see the United States adopt the census categories used in Canada. "My feeling is if we move to the Canadian model, which is multiple boxes . . . [people] can check off however many apply and still have their numbers count. . . ." In Daniel's view a multiracial category would not provide information about a person's heritage in traditional racial or ethnic terms.[5]

Nevertheless, according to Edwin Darden, a regional vice president of the AMEA, "The interracial community has chosen 'Biracial/Multiracial' as the positive, accurate racial designation for a person whose parents are of different races. That description allows children to claim both heritages and fosters a confident sense of self."[6]

But some multiracial people oppose both the multiracial and the multiple classification designations, preferring instead an identity such as Asian, Native American, Black, or Latino. Individuals choose a monoracial identity because that is the way they see themselves, as a number of interviewees have indicated in comments included throughout this book. Others believe that their psychological and even physical well-being depends on such an identity, particularly when they feel pressured or intimidated by peer groups (such as in school or the workplace) to make a monoracial choice. Still others are concerned that increasing the number of ways to classify people will only result in a system that will further divide and alienate racial and ethnic groups in the United States.

Various single-race groups oppose a multiracial classification because they fear their numbers will diminish if people are not counted and classified in traditional categories. Opponents say a reduction in the members of currently accepted racial groups could mean diminished political and social clout. Political boundaries in states and regions and federal and state funding for various educational and social programs depend on monoracial classifications.

However, numerous mixed-race people say they have never wanted to take away resources that might be allocated to someone else or to undermine civil rights gains. Some racially mixed individuals say they would reconsider their efforts to be counted in a multiracial category if such a count had an adverse impact on another minority group.

[109]

CHANGING CLASSIFICATIONS

Advocates of change say that if individuals are going to be truthful about their heritage and statisticians are going to compile accurate data, then records should reflect that some people are part of more than one racial group. Two national organizations working toward that goal are AMEA and Project RACE (Reclassify All Children Equally).

AMEA was founded in 1988 in Berkeley, California, and is a confederation of interracial and multiethnic groups from across the United States. Its purpose is "to promote a positive awareness of interracial and multiethnic identity, for ourselves and for society as a whole." In mid-1992, the organization called for an immediate change in racial categories, but at the same time noted that AMEA "abhors the use of racial statistics for official record-keeping." Recognizing, however, that "the use of race classifications is pervasive and entrenched as part of law, custom or government policy" in the United States, AMEA urged that "the innocuous and degrading 'Other' category" be eliminated. In the summer of 1993, a U.S. House Subcommittee held hearings on "Government Measurement of Race and Ethnicity," and invited several members of the mixed-race community to appear. In her testimony, AMEA president Ramona Douglass argued that

> *If America was living up to its ideals, which advocate equality for all, in the eyes of the law, maybe racial classifications of any kind would be unnecessary, and we would simply acknowledge people ethnically, as Americans first and foremost. But the ideal has yet to become the reality. Those of us in the national, multicultural community firmly believe that "race" or "ethnic"*

affiliation is a personal choice, and should not be in the public, political or governmental domain. As long as it is, multiracial/multiethnic children have the right to be identified as just that: "multiracial/multiethnic."[7]

AMEA has advocated a form that would include not only a multiracial category but also a "Hispanic/Latino" category with boxes to indicate "Mexican/Latino/Chicano," "Puerto Rican," "Cuban," or "Other Country of Origin." The varied terms under Hispanic/Latino are important because, as Carlos Fernandez, former president of AMEA, explained: "'Hispanic' is as much of a misnomer when applied to Latin Americans as 'Anglo' is when applied to most North Americans. Not only are very few Latin Americans actually from Spain the vast majority are of mixed ethnic and 'racial' ancestry and culture."[8]

Project RACE, which was founded in 1991 by members of the Interracial Family Alliance of Atlanta (IFAA), Georgia, is organized separately from IFAA in order to concentrate on school classification systems. "We formed because so many biracial or multiracial teenagers were upset that there was no place for them to indicate their identity on achievement tests and application forms for college," explained Susan Graham, executive director. She is the mother of two biracial children (Graham is white and her husband is black). "It's important for the self-esteem of a multiracial child to be able to indicate his or her true identity," she said, pointing out that her preteenage son "is labeled black at school, white on Census Bureau forms, and biracial at home."[9]

In the early 1990s, Project RACE successfully brought about changes in several Georgia school districts, and after a three-year effort, the Georgia legislature unanimously passed a law that requires a multiracial category on all state forms. Not long after its inception, the organization also began to work nationwide to help introduce similar bills in other states. Ohio and Illinois have passed laws mandating a multiracial category on government forms, and similar legislation is pending in other states.

State legislators have been highly cooperative and supportive, Graham said. "Generally the reaction has been: 'It's about time'" that multiracial people are counted and recognized. Other successful efforts of Project RACE have included community education programs and conferences with medical personnel, calling attention to the needs of multiracial people. "Parents of biracial or multiracial children and multiracial people from all across the United States tell us how pleased they are about some of the positive changes that are taking place. They no longer feel alone," Graham said.[10]

While multiracial groups continue to press their case for new census categories, the U.S. Office of Management and Budget held a series of hearings during the summer of 1994 to reconsider its classification system, which is used as the standard for other government offices. Some possible changes could include the addition of a "Multiracial" category, a change from a "Black" category to "African-American" and "American Indian or Alaska Native" category to "Native American." The category "Hispanic" might be converted to a racial group (rather than ethnic), and a new group might be added for Middle Easterners, who are now categorized as "White."[11]

BUILDING BRIDGES

Educational programs that recognize the contributions of multiracial people as well as the contributions of monoracial groups can build bridges between people.

Such educational efforts may be initiated in schools, government offices, health-care facilities, and other institutions in a community. However, most multicultural programs focus on distinct cultures and almost always ignore blended cultures and people who represent racial mixtures. Yet multicultural programs can at least introduce a perspective other than that of the dominant white viewpoint, focusing on accomplishments of various minority groups rather than downgrading others' heritage as has often been true in the past. As Patsy Clark of Pawnee and European ancestry and instructor at Indiana University, South Bend, noted:

For centuries, white Europeans have believed and taught untruths about the people [Native Americans]. Just recently I had a confrontation with the Indiana Department of Education because they had prepared a Native American module—an instruction sheet for teachers—and it was garbage, with absolutely no truth in history. What they attempted to teach about the culture was incredibly ignorant. For example, rather than describe the forced removal of the people from their land, the module called this a "migration," implying that it was voluntary. When I asked why they did not want to teach that Native Americans had been driven from their land, the woman who had prepared the module said that "children should not be taught that"—about white brutality, I assume. Another example: when I explained that until 1978 Native Americans were not allowed to practice their religion, the woman asked: "Why was that, were they doing drugs?" With such prejudicial attitudes, how can the truth be taught?[12]

Unfortunately, many white Americans may never feel a need to acknowledge or even be aware that a pattern of living other than that of the mainstream can be worthwhile. At the same time, some people who are part of a nonwhite racial group may spend most of their lives with only those who share their particular culture, never having any more than superficial contact with other groups or even with the larger society.

But the United States is made up of diverse cultures, and each has contributed to the total society. People can unite and blend without destroying values of individual cultures. So does a multiracial American or member of an interracial family play a role in the task of building bridges across racial boundaries?

The answer varies with individuals. Certainly some take part in educational efforts and also efforts to ensure that multiracial people are represented in an accurate way in the popular media and in educational materials. Others feel they are "making a statement" about respect for diversity just by existing. In Santa Monica, California, teenager Joshua Bozman of black/white ancestry is hopeful as are many other Americans that someday racial categories will no longer be necessary. But first society has to "admit that multiracial people do exist," he stated. "Then if we all stop seeing each other as just Black, White, Latino, etc., we will be able to show the world that it is possible to live together in harmony."[13]

Bozman's view has been echoed by many individuals of mixed ancestry. They believe they are in a unique position to make a difference in how people from diverse groups see one another, since they are the offspring of people who appreciated diversity and bridged the gaps between racial groups. They demonstrate togetherness, not separatism, and want to embrace and celebrate all of who they are.

APPENDIX

INTERRACIAL SUPPORT GROUPS

NATIONAL

A Place for Us
(28 locations nationwide)
P.O. Box 357
Gardena, CA 90248-7857
(213) 779-1717

Association of Multi-Ethnic
    Americans
P.O. Box 191726
San Francisco, CA 94119-1726
(510) 523-AMEA

Internet/E-mail address:
Internet amea@sgi.com

International Institute for the
   Healing of Racism
Route 113, Box 232
Thetford, VT 05074
(802) 785-2627

PROJECT RACE
1425 Market Blvd. Ste 1320-E6
Roswell, GA 30076
(404) 640-7100

THE SOUTH

Interracial Family Circle
P.O. Box 53290
Washington, DC 20009
(703) 719-9887

BRANCH (Biracial and Natural Children)
P.O. Box 50051
Lighthouse Point, FL 33074
(305) 781-6798

Tallahassee Multiracial Connection
2001 Holmes St.
Tallahassee, FL 32310
(904) 576-6734

Harmony
P.O. Box 16996
W. Palm Beach, FL 33416

Interracial Family Alliance
c/o Tonia and Glenn Thomas
P.O. Box 82105

Athens, GA 30605
(706) 353-0640

Interracial Family Alliance
P.O. Box 20290
Atlanta, GA 30325
(404) 696-8113

Interracial Family Alliance
P.O. Box 9117
Augusta, GA 30906
(706) 793-8547

Northern Kentucky Multiracial Alliance
Pat DiMartile
P.O. Box 175784
Covington, KY 41017-9998
(606) 331-2373

Brick by Brick Ministry
1018 New Circle Rd.
Lexington, KY 40505

Interracial Ministries of America
5805 Aqua Court
Charlotte, NC 28215

Knoxville Interracial Network
attn: Diana Schooler
2234 Martin L. King Blvd.
Knoxville, TN 37915

Mid South Interracial Interaction Assoc.
Rick and Sara Clayton
7272 Mountain Ash
Memphis, TN 38125

Interracial Family and
   Social Alliance of D/FW
P.O. Box 35109
Dallas, TX, 75235-0109
(214) 559-6929

Mixers
P.O. Box 36424
Dallas, Texas 75235
(214) 902-0060

Interracial Family Alliance
P.O. Box 16248
Houston, TX, 77222
(713) 454-5018

Center for the Healing of Racism
P.O. Box 27327
Houston, TX 77227
(713) 526-RACE

Interracial Connection
P.O. Box 7055
Norfolk, VA 23509
(804) 622-9260

THE NORTHEAST

Multiracial Family Group
Network of Culture Sharing Inc.
P.O. Box 554
Boston, MA 02258
(617) 332-6241

Students of Mixed Heritage
c/o Jonathan Kelley

SU 2303 Williams College
Williamstown, MA 01267
(413) 597-6063

GIFT of Lakewood, NJ
P.O. Box 811
Lakewood, NJ 08701
Call Sandy Scott at (908) 364-8136
or Betty Turko at (908) 367-2755

Interracial Club of Buffalo
P.O. Box 400 (Amherst Branch)
Buffalo, NY 14226
(716) 875-6958

Multiracial Americans of N.Y.
c/o Lyn Jordan
Zeckendorf Towers
111 E. 14th St. Suite 219
New York, NY 10003

Council on Interracial
  Books for Children
1841 Broadway
New York, NY 10023
(212) 757-5339

Rainbow Circle
Broadfield Assoc.
P.O. Box 242
Chester, PA 19016

Interracial Families, Inc.
5450 Friendship Ave.
Pittsburgh, PA 15232
(412) 362-0221

SOME Families
1798 Unionville-Lenape Rd.
West Chester, PA 19382
(215) 793-1533

THE MIDWEST

Biracial Family Network
P.O. Box 3214
Chicago, IL 60654-0214
(312) 288-3644

Families for Interracial Awareness
Northern Chicago area
Linda Thomas
(708) 869-7117

Tapestry c/o Sherry Blass
40 Francis Ave.
Crystal Lake, IL 60014

Dialogue Racism Inc.
(chapters nationwide)
Charles Young
P.O. Box 110
Evanston, IL 60204
(708) 492-0123

Interracial Family Network
P.O. Box 5380
Evanston, IL 60204-5830

Child International
4121 Crestwood
Northbrook, IL 60062

Adoptive Parents Together
Linda Russo
427 N. Wheaton Ave.
Wheation, IL 60187

North Shore Race Unity Task Force
536 Sheridan Rd.
Wilmette, IL 60091

Multiracial Group at the University
    of Michigan, Ann Arbor
Karen Downing
(313) 747-3690

Multi Racial Family and
    Youth Network
c/o Juanita Summers
P.O. Box 7521
Bloomfield Hills, MI 48302
(313) 335-7629

Society for Interracial Families
P.O. Box 4942
Troy, MI 48099
(313) 643-6652

Interracial Family Unity Network
Diana Page
1015 Dulle St.
Jefferson City, MO 65109-5276

Multiracial Family Circle
4801 Main
P.O. Box 32414
Kansas City, MO 64171

Cleveland Area Interracial Families
c/o Michael and Joylyn Schweglar
P.O. Box 19258
Cleveland, OH 44119
(216) 371-4717

SWIRLS Ministry
Bob and Gerry Schneider
132 E. South St.
Fostoria, OH 44830

Interracial Family Association
c/o Reginald Saxton
P.O. Box 34323
Parma, OH 44134
216-348-3500

Rainbow Families of Toledo
(adoption support group)
Nancy Shanks
1920 S. Shore Blvd.
Oregon, OH 43618
(419) 693-9259

The Heights Multicultural Group
c/o Sylvia Billups
South Euclid, OH 44121
(216) 382-7912

Cincinnati Multicultural Alliance
P.O. Box 17163
St. Bernard, OH 45217
(513) 791-6023

Interracial Family Support Network
2120 Fordem Ave.

Madison, WI 53704
(608) 241-5150

Multiracial Alliance of Wisconsin
P.O. Box 9122
Madison, WI 53715
(608) 256-0398

THE WEST

Multiracial Americans of Southern
 California (MASC)
12228 Venice Blvd., #452
Los Angeles, CA 90066
(310) 836-1535

National Association for the
 Unity of Mixed-Race People
P.O. Box 4075
Orange, CA 92668

RACE UNITY—MATTERS!
 of Northern California
4309 Linda Vista Ave.
Napa, CA 94558

IMAGE
P.O. Box 4432
San Diego, CA 92164
(619) 527-2850

Interracial Intercultural Pride
(I-Pride) Inc.
P.O. Box 191752
San Francisco, CA 94119-1752
(510) 653-1929

F.C. Communique
P.O. Box 478
Fort Collins, CO 80522

Honor Our New Ethnic Youth (HONEY)
454 Willamette Ave.
Eugene, OR 97401
(503) 342-3908

Interrracial Family Network
P.O. Box 12505
Portland, OR 97212

Interracial Network
P.O. Box 344
Auburn, WA 98071-0344

CANADA

New Brunswick Mulatto
Group, Inc.
P.O. Box 4353
Dieppe, N.B. E1A6E9

FREE CORRESPONDENCE CLUBS

Interracial Lifestyle Connection
4406 N. 54th St.
Fort Smith, AR 72904

Alliance Beyond Color
(Children's pen pals)
P.O. Box 74
Stanton, CA 90680

SOURCE NOTES

CHAPTER ONE

1.   Kathy Kemp, "ReVonda Bowen Speaks Out," *New People* (May/June 1994), p. 12. Also: Southern Poverty Law Center, "Center Sues Principal and School Board for Violation of Student's Civil Rights," *SPLC Report* (July 1994), p. 1 and p. 6.

2.   Southern Poverty Law Center, "Center Sues Principal and School Board for Violation of Student's Civil Rights," *SPLC Report* (July 1994), p. 6.

3.   Personal correspondence and interviews with teenagers in March, April, and May 1993.

4.   Personal interviews with Veronica and Victoria, May 9, 1992.

5.   Personal correspondence, April 27, 1993.

6.   Personal interview, October 4, 1992.

7.   Personal interview, August 25, 1992.

8.   Maria P.P. Root, ed., *Racially Mixed People in America* (Newbury Park, Calif.: Sage Publications, 1992), p. 3.

9.   Paul R. Spickard, "The Illogic of American Racial Categories," in Maria P.P. Root, ed., *Racially Mixed People in America* (Newbury Park, Calif., and London: Sage Publications, 1992), p. 13.

10.   Gordon W. Allport, *The Nature of Prejudice*, 10th edition, (Reading, Mass.: Addison-Wesley Publishing Company, 1979), p. 113.

CHAPTER TWO

1.   Paul R. Spickard, "The Illogic of American Racial Categories," in Maria P.P. Root, ed., *Racially Mixed People in America* (Newbury Park, Calif., and London: Sage Publications, 1992), p. 19.

2.   Michael Banton, *Racial and Ethnic Competition* (Cambridge, Mass., and London: Cambridge University Press, 1983), p. 51.

3.   Quoted in John Catalinotto, "Racism, Genetics and the Roots of Crime," *Workers World Service* electronic news transfer (September 20, 1992). Also: Asia Toufexis, "Seeking the Roots of Violence," *Time* (April 19, 1993), p. 52.

4.   Ibid.

5.   William Loren Katz, *Black Indians: A Hidden Heritage* (New York: Atheneum, 1986), p. 3. Also Katz, "The Americas' First Rainbow Coalition," *Interrace* (March/April 1992), p. 35.

6.   Irving Lewis Allen, *The Language of Ethnic Conflict* (New York: Columbia University Press, 1983), p. 107.

CHAPTER THREE

1.   Allison Joseph, "The Effects of Racism on White-Appearing Children of Integrated Marriages," *Interrace* (May-June 1992), pp. 28-32.

2.   Quoted in Robert Anthony Watts, "Not Black, Not

[126]

White, But Biracial Mixed-Race People Questioning Labels," *Atlanta Constitution* (December 1, 1991), p. A1.

3. Comments during "Into the Mix" forum, Berkeley, California, March 13, 1993.

4. Quoted in Dexter Waugh, "Multiracial Students Search for Identity," *San Francisco Examiner* (April 21, 1991), p. B5.

5. From an address by Terry Wilson at the sixth annual Kaleidoscope conference, Los Angeles, Calif., October 17, 1992.

6. Michelle M. Motoyoshi, "The Experience of Mixed-Race People: Some Thoughts and Theories," *The Journal of Ethnic Studies*, Summer 1990, pp 83-84.

7. Ibid., pp. 87-88.

8. Elizabeth Atkins, "If Looks Could Kill," *New People* (September/October 1992), pp. 10-13.

9. Kathy Russell, Midge Wilson, and Ronald Hall, *The Color Complex: The Politics of Skin Color Among African Americans* (New York: Harcourt Brace Jovanovich, 1992), pp. 4-6.

10. "Why Skin Color Suddenly Is a Big Issue Again," *Ebony* (March 1992), pp. 120-121.

11. Quoted in "How Black is Black?" *Boston Globe* (January 19, 1993), Living Section, p. 51.

12. Kathy Russell, Midge Wilson, and Ronald Hall, *The Color Complex: The Politics of Skin Color Among African Americans* (New York: Harcourt Brace Jovanovich, 1992), pp. 166.

13. Hal Glatzer, "The Melting Pot in the Hawaiian Sun," *San Francisco Chronicle* (December 29, 1991), This World section, p. 16Z.

14. Ronald C. Johnson, "Offspring of Cross-Race and Cross-Ethnic Marriages in Hawaii," in Maria P.P. Root, ed., *Racially Mixed People in America* (Newbury Park, Calif.: Sage Publications, 1992), p. 243.

15. Jill Smolowe, "Intermarried . . . with Children," *Time* (special issue, Fall 1993), p. 64.

CHAPTER FOUR

1. Personal interview, October 4, 1992.
2. Quoted in Leslie Juniel, "Everything Is Not Black or White," *Rocky Mountain News* (July 26, 1990), Lifestyles p. 73.
3. Henry Bramwell, "Choose or Lose," Letter to the Editor column, *Interrace* (September/October, 1991), p. 5.
4. Adham Sawaad, correspondence with the author, April 19, 1993.
5. Wei Bie Chuan, "Dissenting from the Interracial Movement: A Chinese-American Perspective," in Margo Hearst, ed., *Interracial Identity: Celebration, Conflict, or Choice?* (Chicago: Biracial Family Network, 1993), pp. 97-99.
6. Michelle Breaux, Letters, *Spectrum* (January/February/March 1993), p. 12.
7. G. Reginald Daniel, "Eurocentricism, Afrocentricism, or 'Holocentricism'?" *Interrace* (May/June 1992), p. 33.
8. Amy Iwasaki Mass, "Interracial Japanese Americans: The Best of Both Worlds or the End of the Japanese American Community?" in Maria P.P. Root, ed., *Racially Mixed People in America* (Newbury Park, Calif.: Sage Publications, 1992), pp. 265-66.
9. Ibid., pp. 266-279.
10. Terry P. Wilson, "Blood Quantum: Native American Mixed Bloods," in Maria P. P. Root, ed., *Racially Mixed People in America* (Newbury Park, Calif.: 1992), p. 109.
11. Ibid., p. 112.
12. Santa Barbara Museum of Natural History, *The*

Chumash People (Santa Barbara, Calif.: Santa Barbara Museum of Natural History, 1989), pp. 7-12.

13. Terry P. Wilson, "Blood Quantum: Native American Mixed Bloods," in Maria P. P. Root, ed., *Racially Mixed People in America* (Newbury Park, Calif. : 1992), pp. 124-25.

14. David R. Stevenson, "Playing the Name Game Gets You Labels, Not Self-Respect," *New People* (Summer 1992), pp. 6-7, 40.

15. Panel discussion, UC Berkeley, March 13, 1993.

16. Brian Harris, "Teen Talk," *New People* (January/February 1994), p. 6.

17. Personal interview, May 7, 1992.

CHAPTER FIVE

1. William Yung, "Dealing with Criticism," Letters to the Editor, *New People* (Summer 1992), p. 4.

2. Rose L. Hedgeman, "Internal and External Stressors of Interracial Marriages," *Interracial/-Intercultural Connection*, January/February 1988, p. 4.

3. Personal interview, June 12, 1992.

4. Celia Cuomo, "'Are You His Mother?'" *I-Pride Newsletter* (July/August 1990), p. 4.

5. "Violent Hate Crime Remains at Record Levels Nationwide," *Intelligence Report* (March 1994), p. 1.

6. Steven A. Chin, "Family Lists KKK Member's Campaign to Drive Them Away," *San Francisco Examiner* (October 15, 1991), p. A1.

7. Elizabeth Bartholet, "Where Do Black Children Belong? The Politics of Race Matching in Adoption," *University of Pennsylvania Law Review* (May 1991), pp. 1211-1212.

8. Personal interview, June 12, 1992.

9. "Civil Rights Office Finds Minnesota Agency To Be In Violation of U.S. Civil Rights Laws," *The Children's Voice* (April/June 1992), p. 1.

10. Tara L. Tieso-Battis, "Adopting A New Point of View," *New People* (Summer 1992), p. 27.

11. Francis Wardle, "Interracial Children and Their Families: How School Social Workers Should Respond," *Social Work in Education* (July 1991), p. 218.

12. Phone interview, March 17, 1993.

13. Quoted in DeNeen L. Brown, "For Mothers of Biracial Children, Prejudice Mars the Pride," *The Washington Post* (May 12, 1991), p. B1.

CHAPTER SIX

1. Maia Benjamin-Wardle, "Pointing Out Differences Simply Furthers the Stereotypes," New People (March/April 1993), p. 8.

2. Ibid.

3. Personal interview, March 13, 1993 and telephone interview, March 16, 1993.

4. Phone interview, April 29, 1993.

5. Phone interview, April 5, 1993.

6. Dickelle Fonda, Letters to the Editor, *Interrace* (March/April 1992), p. 32.

7. Mary Murchison-Edwords, "'Mixed' Movies List," 1992.

8. Phone interview, March 25, 1993.

9. Quoted in Candy Mills, "Mira Nair," *Interrace* (May/June 1992), p. 9.

10. Quoted in Yvette Walker Hollis, "Cover Story—Giancarlo Esposito," *New People* (January/February 1993), p. 11.

11. Ibid.

CHAPTER SEVEN

1. Carlos Fernandez, "Much of the World Is an Ethnic Melting Pot," *San Jose Mercury News*, Editorial Page, (October 6, 1989), p. 8B.

2. News Section, "Update Germany 2 Years After Unification," *San Francisco Chronicle* (October 6, 1992), p. A7.
3. Chronicle Wire Services, "Germany Divided Over Anti-Violence Rally," *San Francisco Chronicle* (November 7, 1992), p. A12.
4. "Eurasian German Man Says Neo-Nazism 'Is Serious'," *I-Pride Newsletter* (December 1992), p. 8.
5. Mark Heinrich, "German Poll Shows Pro-Nazi Views," Reuters News Service story published in a variety of newspapers (November 7, 1992).
6. Quoted in Yasmin Alibhai Brown and Anne Montague, "Choosing Sides," *New Statesman & Society* (February 7, 1992), p. 15.
7. Colin Nickerson and Junko Fujita, "In Japan, 'Different' Is Dangerous," *Boston Globe* (January 24, 1993), National/Foreign Section, p. 1.
8. Teresa Williams, "An Amerasian Identity," *Interrace* (March-April 1991), p. 10.
9. Kieu-Linh Caroline Valverde, "From Dust to Gold: The Vietnamese Amerasian Experience," in Maria P. P. Root, ed., *Racially Mixed People in America* (Newbury Park, Calif.: Sage Publications, 1992), p. 144.
10. Ibid., p. 160.
11. Jan Robyn Weisman, "'Half Children': A History of Racial Mixing and Racially Mixed Individuals in Thailand," in Margo Hearst, ed., *Interracial Identity: Celebration, Conflict, or Choice?*, pp. 34-36.

CHAPTER EIGHT

1 Quoted in Jerry Holderman, "'Colorblind' Boy Shares His Place," *Los Angeles Times* (October 14, 1992), Part E, p. 3.
2. Brian Harris, "Friendship Sees No Color," press release, April 1993.
3. Quoted in Khikiri Hightower, "Mixed Students

[131]

Succeed at BHS," *Berkeley High Jacket* (September 25, 1992), p. 1.

4. Phone interviews, March 21 and May 3, 1993.

5. Ibid.

6. Joan Walsh, "'You Can See the World in Their Faces,'" *Image* (February 9, 1992), p. 10.

7. Quoted in Elizabeth Atkins, "Students of Mixed Race Form Bond," *St. Louis Post Dispatch* (June 25, 1991), p. 1D.

8. Personal interview, March 12, 1993.

9. Presentation during panel discussion, "Into the Mix" forum, Berkeley, California, March 13, 1993.

10. Comment during panel discussion "Into the Mix" forum, Berkeley, California, March 13, 1993.

11. Phone interview, March 22, 1993.

12. Ibid.

13. Comment during a general discussion after "Into the Mix" forum, Berkeley, California, March 13, 1993.

14. Ibid.

15. Comments during Kaleidoscope conference, Los Angeles, California, October 17, 1992.

16. Personal interview, March 13, 1993.

CHAPTER NINE

1. Kent D. Syverud, "The Census Frowns on Mixed Marriages, Mixed-Race Kids," *Detroit Free Press* (April 11, 1990), p. 7A.

2. Quoted in John Balzar, "Biracial Families See a Road to Equality Paved with Diversity," *Los Angeles Times* (October 7, 1992), p. A5.

3. Quoted in Jason Sperber, "Not One Or the Other: Teens Want Their Multiracial Identities to Be Recognized," *LA Youth* (September/October 1991), p. 10.

4. Ibid., p. 11.

5. Quoted in Elizabeth Campos Rajs, "Pros, Cons of Ethnic Labels," *UC Focus* (May/June 1991), p. 8.

6. Personal interview, March 29, 1993.

7. Ramona Douglass, Prepared statement presented to the Subcommittee on Census, Statistics & Postal Personnel, June 20, 1993.

8. Carlos Fernandez, "Much of the World Is an Ethnic Melting Pot," *San Jose Mercury News,* Editorial Page, (October 6, 1989), p. 8B.

9. Phone interview, April 5, 1993.

10. Ibid.

11. Carrie Teegardin, "Mixed-Parentage Gap," *Atlanta Constitution* (July 7, 1994), p. A4.

12. Personal interview, April 12, 1993.

13. Personal correspondence, April 23, 1993.

BIBLIOGRAPHY

Alba, Richard D., ed. *Ethnicity and Race in the U.S.A.* New York and London: Routledge, Chapman & Hall, 1988.

Allen, Irving Lewis. *The Language of Ethnic Conflict*. New York: Columbia University Press, 1983.

Becker, John T., and Stanli K. Becker. *All Blood Is Red, All Shadows Are Dark*. Cleveland, Oh.: Seven Shadows Press, 1984.

Boyer, James B. *Curriculum Materials for Ethnic Diversity*. Lawrence, Kans.: Center for Black Leadership Development and Research, 1990.

Bunzel, John H. *Race Relations on Campus: Stanford Students Speak*. Stanford, Calif.: The Portable Stanford Book Series, 1992.

Davis, F. James. *Who Is Black? One Nation's Definition*. University Park, Pa.: Pennsylvania State University 1991.

Funderburg, Lise. *Black, White, Other*. New York: William Morrow and Co., 1993.

Gay, Kathlyn. *Bigotry*. Hillside, N.J.: Enslow Publishers, 1989.

Gay, Kathlyn. *The Rainbow Effect: Interracial Families*. New York: Franklin Watts, 1987.

Harrington, Walt. *Crossings: A White Man's Journey Into Black America*. New York: HarperCollins, 1993.

Hearst, Margo Ruark, ed. *Interracial Identity: Celebration, Conflict, or Choice?* Chicago, Ill.: Biracial Family Network, 1993.

Hoffman, Paul, ed. "The Science of Race." Special Issue, *Discover,* November 1994.

Katz, William Loren. *Black Indians: A Hidden Heritage*. New York: Atheneum, 1986.

Katz, William Loren, and Paula A. Franklin. *Proudly Red and Black: Stories of Native and African Americans*. New York: Macmillan, 1993.

Lardner, Joyce A. *Mixed Families: Adoption Across Racial Boundaries*. New York: Anchor Press/Doubleday, 1977.

Locke, Don C. *Increasing Multicultural Understanding*. Newbury Park, Calif.: Sage Publications, 1992.

No Collective, ed. *Voices of Identity, Rage and Deliverance: An Anthology of Writings by People of Mixed Descent*. Oakland, Calif.: No Press, 1992.

Review of Federal Measurements of Race and Ethnicity. Washington, D.C.: U.S. Government Printing Office, 1994.

Root, Maria P.P., ed. *Racially Mixed People in America*. Newbury Park, Calif.: Sage Publications, 1992.

Snowden, Frank M. *Before Color Prejudice: The Ancient View of Blacks*. Cambridge, Mass.: Harvard University Press, 1983.

Spickard, Paul R. *Mixed Blood: Intermarriage and Ethnic Identity in Twentieth-Century America*. Madison, Wis.: The University of Wisconsin Press, 1989.

Terkel, Studs. *Race: How Blacks and Whites Think and Feel About The American Obsession*. New York: Doubleday, 1992.

"The New Face of America." Special Issue *Time Magazine*, Fall 1993.

Tizard, Barbara, and Ann Phoenix. *Black, White, or Mixed Race? Race and Racism in the Lives of Young People of Mixed Parentage*. New York and London: Routledge, Chapman & Hall, 1993.

Wilson, Anne. *Mixed Race Children: A Study of Identity*. New York: Routledge, Chapman & Hall, 1987.

Zack, Naomi. *Race and Mixed Race*. Philadelphia, Pa.: Temple University Press, 1993.

INDEX

National Coalition to End Racism in America's Child Care System (NCERACCS), 66
Native Americans, 25–26, 52–55, 113
Nature of Prejudice, The (Allport), 18
Neo-Nazis, 84–86
New People: The Journal for the Human Race, 17

O'Leary, Hazel, 79
One-drop of blood rule, 30, 48, 50

Parenting strategies, 69–70
Pen-pal clubs, 95–96
Philippines, 92–93
Power and racial classifications, 18
Pozzo, Bryan, 108
Project RACE, 110–112
Public curiosity, 60
Public forums, 96–98

Race category on census forms, 107–109
Racially Mixed People in America (Root), 17
Ramos, Fidel, 93
Randolph County High School (Alabama), 11–13
Religion, 22, 27
Research, racism supported by, 19, 22–24, 31–32
Root, Maria, 16
Roseno, Hartho T., 85

Schools and multiracial relationships, 11–13, 99–102
Science, 27
Self-identity
    census forms, 107–109
    choosing a single-race category, 48–53, 55–57
    embracing all of one's multiracial heritage, 70
    ongoing process, 47–48
social workers/clinicians influencing, 97
    transracial adoptees, 65
Selling out to the white culture, 50–51
Seneviratne, Denise, 86–87
Serbians, 84

Slavery, 21–22, 25
Social workers/clinicians, 97
South Africa, 82–83
Southern Poverty Law Center, 12–13, 61

[143]